THE
STEWARDESS IS
FLYING THE PLANE!

THE
STEWARDESS IS
FLYING THE PLANE!

AMERICAN FILMS OF THE 1970s

RON HOGAN

A CONVERSATION WITH PETER BOGDANOVICH

MANOAH BOWMAN, PHOTO EDITOR

BULFINCH PRESS
NEW YORK   BOSTON

CONTENTS

BLACK SUNDAY

Bruce Dern as a crazed Vietnam vet who flies the Goodyear blimp into the Super Bowl in *Black Sunday* (1977).

Bogdanovich filming *What's Up, Doc?* (1972).

A Conversation with Peter Bogdanovich

It is impossible to talk about the movies of the 1970s without working your way around to Peter Bogdanovich. His directing career actually began in 1968, with the low-budget thriller *Targets*, but it was his second film, *The Last Picture Show*, that really kicked his reputation into high gear. Shot for just over $1 million, the movie was released in the fall of 1971 and earned eight Academy Award nominations, with Ben Johnson and Cloris Leachman taking home acting Oscars; Bogdanovich himself was nominated as the film's director and co-author of the screenplay adapted from Larry McMurtry's novel. His next film, *What's Up, Doc?*, was one of the biggest hits of 1972, while the film after that, *Paper Moon*, was nominated for four Oscars, with Tatum O'Neal becoming the youngest actress to receive the prize in competition. After poorly received forays into musicals and costume dramas, Bogdanovich returned to his roots with the solidly crafted, low-budget films *Saint Jack* (1979) and *They All Laughed* (1981) and went on to direct the critically acclaimed *Mask* in 1985.

Bogdanovich has continued to direct movies over the last twenty years, but he has also had great success returning to his professional origins as a film journalist and historian through books such as *Who the Devil Made It: Conversations with Legendary Film Directors* and *Who the Hell's in It: Portraits and Conversations*. Because of Bogdanovich's central role as both a participant and chronicler of Hollywood's legacy, I was quite grateful for the opportunity to meet with him at his Manhattan apartment in the winter of 2004 to discuss the era of the "new Hollywood" in the 1970s and his role in it.

RH: How did the Hollywood revolution of the 1970s begin?

PB: Well, the old studio system, which involved contract players and everybody being under contract, completely fell apart by about 1962. I always sort of date it from around the time when Warner Bros. disbanded their cartoon division, killing Bugs Bunny. A dark period followed for five or six years, where there wasn't really much interesting happening—the Beatles had arrived, and records were more compelling than movies. Then in '67 *Bonnie and Clyde* came along, which Arthur Penn directed. He wasn't really a new director; he was from the Frankenheimer/Lumet generation. But Warren Beatty was pushing that new direction. The studio didn't like it, but it became a hit. Then in '68, when I made *Targets*, there was John Cassavetes's *Faces* and Scorsese's first film, *Who's That*

TARGETS

Boris Karloff (left) and Bogdanovich during the filming of *Targets* (1968).

Knocking at My Door? Faces was a huge success financially, and then in '69, *Easy Rider*, and in 1970, *Five Easy Pieces.*

But it really started in 1970 with Paramount. They had a number of huge pictures, each of them costing $25 million, which in those days was a lot of money — *On a Clear Day You Can See Forever*, *The Molly Maguires*, and *Paint Your Wagon*—and all of them tanked. But then there were movies like *Easy Rider*, which cost less than a million and made a fortune, and in 1966, Roger

Corman's *Wild Angels*, which I worked on, that cost $300,000 and grossed $6 million. That was revealing to the studios, and they thought that maybe big blockbusters were not the way to go. That was probably one of the few times in the history of movies where the studios didn't know what to do, and they thought, well, these guys seem to have their finger on some kind of pulse, let's go with that. So there was a brief moment when a large box-office gross was considered possible for pictures that didn't cost a lot of money. The unions even created kind of a special rate—if you made the picture for $1 million or less, you didn't have to take as many people with you. *Picture Show* fell into that category. It's one of the reasons it got made the way it got made. That doesn't exist today. That whole way of thinking that small can equal big was great.

It was also a time when the attention was put on the director as superstar. The director could be the artist, could lead the way. I remember I made a joke at the time of *Easy Rider*, that the easiest way to get to direct a picture was to never have directed one, and I think that was true for a few years. It's not the case now.

RH: What is the first memory that springs to mind when you look back at the late 1960s and early 1970s?

PB: The first thing I remember is preparing to make *Picture Show* in late '69, early '70. I'd been in Rome, preparing a picture that I never made, with Sergio Leone, called *Duck, You Sucker—A Fistful of Dynamite* was the final title. Sergio ended up making it himself, which is what I suspected would happen. So I came back for Christmas in '69 and went right to work preparing *The Last Picture Show*. Almost all of '70 prior to shooting was spent casting, rewriting, and preparing the script, and everything else you do on a picture.

RH: Looking back at *The Last Picture Show* today, younger viewers might look at that cast and think, My God, how did he get all these stars in it? At the time, though, very few of them were the stars they are now.

PB: Except for Ben Johnson, nobody was known. Cloris Leachman had been seen on series television, and Tim Bottoms did one movie that was being shot in '70, *Johnny Got His Gun*. But Ellen Burstyn, Eileen Brennan, and Jeff Bridges had only been in a few small things, and Cybill Shepherd and Randy Quaid had never even been in a picture. We talked about maybe having some stars. I met with Vera Miles about playing one of those women and talked about Jimmy Stewart playing Ben Johnson's part, but at some point we all agreed that, since it's a small town in Texas, there shouldn't be any stars in it, so the intention was pretty much to find people without names.

Ben Johnson was really my first and only choice for Sam the Lion, but he turned it down two or three times because he said there were too many words. I finally called John Ford, who told me, "Aw, he always says that." So I got Ford to call Ben, and Ford scared him to death by telling him, "Do you want to play Duke's sidekick for the rest of your life?" But that still didn't do it. So Orson Welles suggested that maybe we could get a country-western singer, an old-timer, to play the part. I went to Nashville to see if that was going to work, and to learn a lot more about country, because I didn't know anything. I interviewed a lot of people in Nashville—Bill Monroe, Roy Acuff, Ernest Tubbs—I also saw Tex Ritter, but that was in L.A., with John Ritter, who was up for the Tim Bottoms part, which is how I became friends with John. But once I got the idea of Ben Johnson, I wouldn't settle for anybody else, and we somehow finally got him.

RH: Looking back at that era, with films like _Last Picture Show_, _Mean Streets_, and many of the others that were coming out, what to you typifies a film of the seventies revolution?

PB: Speaking for myself, it was the use of essentially classic American narrative film technique but not looking at things in a conventional, cleaned-up way. Certainly _Mean Streets_ was a different kind of gangster picture than we'd seen before. And _Picture Show_ and _Paper Moon_ both had somewhat of an anti-Hollywood approach. In _Picture Show_ I attempted to tell the truth about this town, these people, these situations, in a way that American films hadn't prior to that, particularly about sex, the parental situation, and the kids/parents interaction. I deal with sex in a comic way, but very explicitly, which hadn't been done. When I look at it today, I think it's pretty surprising.

In _Paper Moon_, Tatum was anything but Shirley Temple—she was the antithesis of her. In fact, it was kind of an anti–Shirley Temple movie in a way. Originally the opening sequence took place in a movie theater, where Tatum's character, Addie, was watching a Shirley Temple movie. And I had already had so much "homage" stuff written about me that I thought, Let's not begin with that, or we'll never recover. Even despite the fact that we didn't do that, one New York critic said it was a homage to Shirley Temple, which was really wrong. But I think, in those two cases, it was an attempt to look at the things from a totally different angle.

But I think that all of us who began at that period, to varying degrees, had a sense of Hollywood history, much more than people today. Francis Coppola and Billy Friedkin and Scorsese and I all had different people we liked in terms of past filmmakers, but we did have a sense of film history as well as film grammar that we drew on. That was part of the dynamic—everybody brought his more modern sensibility to bear, but it was definitely based on a kind of technique, a filmmaking technique that was tried and true.

RH: At the very beginning of your career, and the careers of many of your directing peers, Roger Corman was willing to give you all a chance by producing your first movies, even up until the late seventies, when Ron Howard did *Grand Theft Auto*.

PB: There is no question that Roger was a very very important figure in the "new Hollywood." Almost everybody had started with him, whether it was Jack Nicholson, Francis Coppola, Marty Scorsese, or Jonathan Demme. And it was part of Roger's whole kit, a kind of guerrilla warfare kind of filmmaking, where you were doing it down and dirty, and if you had to steal it, you had to steal it. If you couldn't get somebody to pay for permission, you had to steal them. It was a general conspiratorial kind of attitude. And I think it was a good way to begin in the movies. I give Roger a lot of credit for taking a chance on me and a lot of other people. He threw you in the water and said swim, and if you swam, it was fine. If you drowned it was fine, too—he would get somebody else to fix it up.

RH: A sense has come down over the years, particularly from some of the popular histories of this era, that you all were a little more tight knit than directors have been since or possibly even were before. Lucas and Coppola were very close, and you were certainly very close to Cassavetes and others. You don't really hear stories today of, say, Quentin Tarantino hanging out with David O. Russell. Was there really that sort of camaraderie or solidarity?

PB: I think there was, in certain instances, like Coppola and Lucas and Spielberg. Maybe it just seems that way now, that we were all close, yet I can't really speak to that, because I wasn't that friendly with anybody particularly. I was close to John Cassavetes, but he was a bit older than I. Francis and Friedkin and I had a company for a few years, but we weren't particularly close. We tried to make the company work, but for a variety of reasons, it didn't. I think there probably was a camaraderie, but it was true in the older days of the studio, too—John Ford was very friendly with Frank Capra and Leo McCarey.

RH: Now, you are usually associated much more with people from earlier generations. Your closest friendships at the time seem to have been with John Ford and Orson Welles.

PB: Yes. And Howard Hawks. I was definitely more in touch with them than I was with my contemporaries. They took to me because they were flattered that I knew their work intimately and was influenced by it. But I was alone in that. I don't think many people hung out with them.

There is a certain irony in the fact that I became associated with the old Hollywood to such a degree that my pictures were thought of as being homages to other directors. It really wasn't true. It wasn't what I was trying to do, and it wasn't what the movies were. But that sort of got to be the standard Bogdanovich review. I of course talked about the older directors a lot in my interviews because I felt that they weren't working as much as they should. We were just starting out, we were just young punks, why were we working and John Ford wasn't? I had this sort of guilty conscience about it, like we should be doing something to help them. So I talked and gave away as much of the credit as possible, as part of the attempt to give credit where credit was due, even if it wasn't due.

RH: Since you were close with Orson during that time, what did he think about the wave of revolutionary films coming along? In many ways I think they at least strove for—if not always achieved—a kind of ideal of honest, independent filmmaking he had worked at throughout his career.

PB: I remember Orson made a disparaging remark at one point in the seventies that the young film-makers are just remaking the films they had liked when they were kids. It wasn't exactly fair, because if they were remaking films, it was from a different point of view.

RH: You all at some point certainly tried your hand at re-creating genres that you had loved growing up.

PB: Genre was definitely an aspect. *The Godfather* was the biggest grosser of '72, and number two was *What's Up, Doc?* And you could say they were both really genre pictures. One was a gangster picture; one was a screwball romantic comedy.

RH: And then the two top grossers of '73 were *The Exorcist* and *The Sting*, again, both genre pictures.

PB: *Picture Show* and *Paper Moon* didn't really fall into a genre, but my first picture, *Targets*, was a genre picture; it was a thriller. And I did try to make a musical and a western, so that was definitely part of what the dynamic was.

RH: It almost seems as if the public perception was that all of these directors were pushing the edges of film expression and while you did so thematically as well, perhaps your execution of traditional film grammar came across as homage to the earlier directors.

PB: To a degree I think that's true, that they only saw the grammar, not the content. Take, for instance, a scene like Sam the Lion's funeral in *Last Picture Show*—a long shot of the funeral and at the end the people break up and start going down the hill. The composition had a lot of sky in it, but Texas has a lot of sky, that's one of the things you notice about Texas. I saved the long shot for the end of the scene, which is something I actually learned from Hitchcock, who would not use establishing shots to establish, because they have no dramatic impact that way. And people called it a Ford shot, because it was a long shot. But John Ford is not the only person who used long shots in his movies! It wasn't a homage, it was just using a classic film technique.

RH: At some point between '75 and '80, maybe closer to '80, the sense of experimentation in the films that got made evaporated.

PB: Well, there were a couple of reasons. *Star Wars* and *Jaws* had an enormous effect. The way *Jaws* was released changed movies in many ways. Look at *Last Picture Show*. It opened in October in one theater in New York, Chicago, and L.A. and played for several months in those theaters before it opened up wider. We were still in the same theaters when the Oscars were announced at the end of January. So word of mouth was very important and was what movies had always been based on—except exploitation movies, which opened and closed as quickly as possible before word of mouth got out about them. But once A-list movies started to be distributed like exploitation movies, everything changed, because things got watered down. The attempt now was not to be different, but to be the same, and I think it had a negative effect on the quality of movies.

But another aspect was that each of us who started making movies in the late sixties, early seventies had a couple of flops. Sometimes we spent too much money, or it was kind of a difficult process, but everybody had his turn at it. Spielberg made *1941*, which was not successful; *Heaven's Gate* was notorious; Francis had *One from the Heart*; Scorsese made *New York, New York*, which wasn't that big a hit; and I had a debacle with *At Long Last Love*. That vulnerability changed the studios' thinking that we were the answer, and they started moving in a different, more conventional direction.

RH: What are some of your favorite films from the seventies?

PB: [laughs] I was busy making pictures at that period—I made six films in six years—so I pretty much stopped going to movies, and I don't think I ever caught up with some of them. I didn't follow the careers of a lot of my contemporaries the way I did when I was learning about films. I liked *Five Easy Pieces* when it came out and was very fond of Bob Rafelson; I also liked *Mean Streets*. I remember when I first met Marty, and he was explaining to me that he had shot some of it like Howard Hawks, and I couldn't quite get that, but he was talking about medium shots. And I love John Cassavetes movies. I had a closeness to John, even though we didn't make films that were even remotely alike. I guess my favorite movie of the seventies was his *A Woman Under the Influence*. I thought it was the most striking work of that period, and I remember being shaken by it. And I really was blown away by *Husbands*, and loved *Minnie and Moskowitz*. I did return to see his films.

RH: Is there any project that you wish you had done or one that you wish you had done differently?

PB: Well, I was offered a lot of pictures that I turned down for various reasons. Doing *The Godfather*, *The Exorcist*, *Chinatown*, *The Last Detail*, *The Way We Were*. And I was originally on *The Getaway*. I was set to do that before *What's Up, Doc?* Steve McQueen saw *Picture Show* and wanted me to direct his next picture, and then decided to do *Junior Bonner* first. And I was working with Walter Hill on *The Getaway*, and I get a call from Robert Evans, followed by a call from McQueen, basically saying they wanted to use Ali McGraw, and I didn't think Ali was right for a Southern barefoot girl. People say I turned *The Godfather* down—the truth is, I didn't even know what it was they were offering me, because I was so quick to say I wasn't interested. They said they had bought a book by Mario Puzo and that they wanted me to direct it. I asked what it was about, and they said, "The Mafia." I said I wasn't interested, and that was that.

The trouble with all of this is that we didn't have enough experience with success to know what to do, how to handle it. I think some of us learn better than others. What I didn't realize was that when you were offered a script, it didn't mean you had to shoot that script. You could change it, alter it, and finesse it. I kind of stuck with the idea that this was what I had to shoot, which was kind of square. So I turned down things I just didn't see. If I had it to do over again, I would have done some of those pictures.

RH: Are there any pictures you wouldn't have made?

PB: I certainly wouldn't have done *Daisy Miller*. It's a good picture, there's nothing wrong with it, in my point of view. It was many years before the Merchant Ivory kind of movie, so it was ahead of its time. The problem with the picture was that I knew when I was making it that it wasn't commercial. I remember when I had a screening at Paramount, and the head of distribution came over to me afterward, and I said, "What did you think?" He said, "It's ok." I said, "That's all you've got to say?" And he said, "What do you want me to say? You're Babe Ruth, and you bunted." If I had known, if I had been smart about things, I wouldn't have done that. I would not have done something so completely uncommercial. Howard Hawks gave me some advice that I wish I had just kept completely. He said, "Peter, make pictures that make money. It's that simple!"

Daisy Miller threw the studio's confidence in me, that I would do a picture like that instead of thinking only in terms of box office. But I wasn't thinking in terms of box office when I made *Picture Show*. I just hoped it would make its money back. And *Daisy*'s failure helped to fuck up the next two pictures. They were both very personal projects; both *At Long Last Love* and *Nickelodeon* were pictures I really wanted to make, and they came out not the way I wanted, for a variety of reasons. And I was very disappointed, which is why I didn't make pictures for almost three years. I was getting offers all the time, I just didn't want to work until I could get back to some kind of sense of basics. It wasn't until I went back to basics on *Saint Jack*, where I consciously went back to try to make pictures exactly the way I wanted to make them without compromises, without recutting it to please a studio. That was a return to form.

RH: Looking back at the decade, do you feel like you and your peers were as revolutionary as people have made you out to be?

PB: It was a strange time. I'm not great at looking back at my own career, but I know that I wasn't as much a part of the revolution—maybe because I was so into the older directors and stars—and I know that we weren't aware of it when it was going on. We weren't thinking we were the "new Hollywood." I remember a moment when Dennis Hopper turned to George Cukor at a dinner party and said, "We're gonna bury you." And George, looking very chic, said, "Yes, yes, of course." But I never thought of it as burying the past, and if anything, I was trying to celebrate the past in my writing. I had learned a lot from the older directors from that foundation of filmmaking that had been the silent era, the first three decades of the talkies. My parents were more traditional in the thought of art as a kind of relay race. We carry the stick for a while, and we pass it along.

PREFACE

Jack Nicholson directing *Goin' South* (1978).

Peter Bogdanovich's introduction underscores an important, yet sometimes underappreciated, aspect of what has come to be regarded as the "new Hollywood" of the 1970s. While one popular view holds up a handful of directors as maverick filmmakers surrounded by junk, the truth is that many of these directors and the pictures they made fell squarely within the studio system. Francis Ford Coppola's *The Godfather* and William Friedkin's *The Exorcist* are powerful, innovative films, but they weren't "maverick" in the same way as John Cassavetes's *A Woman Under the Influence* or John Waters's *Pink Flamingos*. While it is not wrong to hold up these—and other studio-made films—as great works of art, their position should be recognized within the vast repertoire of Hollywood films from the decade. Too often, people dismiss seventies films for being "genre" or celebrate them only for their alleged "camp" value, evidence of a nationwide lack of taste. Even blaxploitation flicks, while rightly heralded as a powerful expression of contemporary African-American attitudes, fall into the trap of being viewed by modern audiences eager to hoot over what people wore back then.

Case in point: the title of this book refers to one of Karen Black's two most famous roles from the seventies, the other being the television movie *Trilogy of Terror*—pretty much what anybody remembers of Karen Black, period. But those campy memories overlook the fact that she was nominated for an Academy Award for her work in *Five Easy Pieces*—a performance that also won her the first of two Golden Globes. In fact, if you look at all her work in the decade—including *Easy Rider, Nashville, The Day of the Locust*, and *Born to Win*—there is no reason to think of Black as anything other than a serious actress. Not every performance was perfect, and even when she was good, some of the films might otherwise be downright awful, but you can say that about anyone, no matter how big a star. (For example, Gene Hackman, who will appear throughout this book, can breathe easier knowing that it skips over the 1969 flop *Marooned*.)

Of course, it can be hard to take some 1970s films seriously; I defy anybody's resistance to camp to persevere against *Myra Breckinridge* or the giant fake bugs in *Empire of the Ants*—but those films, and dozens more like them, got made for a reason, and this book is as much about those reasons as about the horrendous fashions and the cheesy special effects.

Recently, cultural critics have been making a case that the 1970s were more radical than the 1960s, as the counterculture increasingly became the culture and concepts such as the sexual revolution and feminist consciousness, along with recreational drugs, took hold in the suburbs. This view dovetails neatly with the common perspective on seventies films, with that handful of great directors depicted as a loose band of outsiders who came to Hollywood and turned the studios upside down with their personal visions, subtly transforming how movies were made and what they were about. This story is not untrue, as far as it goes, but it should go further.

In the first "golden age" of Hollywood cinema, each studio could be counted on to deliver a certain type of product. MGM had the biggest stars and the highest budgets, Warner Bros. specialized in gritty melodramas, and so on. That all changed beginning in 1948, when the Supreme Court forced the major studios to relinquish their investments in the movie theater business and broke the corporate lock on the industry. By the 1970s, studios were doing less actual film production themselves and increasingly acting like banks for an assortment of independent production companies, many of them formed by actors or directors who in the old days would have spent their entire careers at one studio. Now, when one studio's investment in a certain type of film paid off, every other studio would frequently scramble to sign up another film just like it.

Hollywood is, after all, a reactive industry; it offers as entertainment what it believes audiences will find entertaining, a principle that holds just as true for low-budget schlock as it does for big-budget masterpieces. The auteurs of the 1970s made huge films about subjects that moved them, issues and events that played out in the headlines, on the nightly news, and even among their own families and friends. Those same issues and events were just as much of an inspiration to independent filmmakers and journeyman holdovers from the classical studio system.

As the mistrust of the status quo that began in the late sixties spread throughout the country, one obvious consequence was an increase in films in which you couldn't trust anyone over thirty, as well as some movies from older filmmakers just as certain you couldn't rely on anyone *under* thirty. But films of the 1970s are about so much more than a simplistic generation gap—they actively encouraged distrust of government and big corporations, cast doubt upon the stability of family and marriage, and suggested that under the right circumstances, even Mother Nature would betray us, so we might as well take matters into our own hands, and if we had to screw somebody over to get what we deserved, well, isn't that just the way life is?

The groundwork for such frank cynicism had been laid in the 1960s, when the studios finally abandoned the Hays Code standards for what could and could not be shown on screen. The Code was not just about naked bodies and obscene language; it had regulated the severity of cinematic violence, firmly enforced a "crime-does-not-pay" ethic, and upheld the sanctity of marriage. Under pressure from the commercial success of more freewheeling European films, Hollywood replaced the Code with a self-imposed ratings system in 1968, and young screenwriters and directors were eager to take advantage of their new freedoms. By 1970, everything and everybody was subject to criticism, and if filmmakers didn't attack a subject directly, they might turn it into the butt of a huge joke.

Of course, as with any rule, there was one huge exception, but that film was set long, long ago, in a galaxy far, far away . . .

SCIENCE FIC

The circle is now complete: Obi-Wan Kenobi confronts his former pupil, Darth Vader, in a pivotal scene from *Star Wars* (1977). British actor David Prowse wore the Vader costume through all three films, though the villain's voice and face were supplied by different actors.

TION

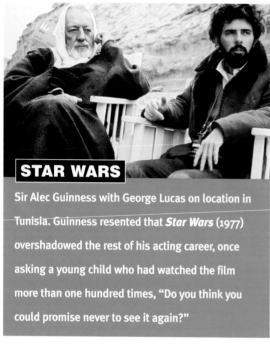

STAR WARS

Sir Alec Guinness with George Lucas on location in Tunisia. Guinness resented that *Star Wars* (1977) overshadowed the rest of his acting career, once asking a young child who had watched the film more than one hundred times, "Do you think you could promise never to see it again?"

Star Wars stood in such stark opposition to the bulk of American films in the 1970s that George Lucas was worried about its potential failure right up until the day in May 1977 when audiences began lining up around the block to see it again and again. In retrospect, his concern is easy to understand; not only did the special effects take forever to get right, his choice of appealing to a younger audience by placing newcomers such as Mark Hamill and Carrie Fisher in key roles meant the film's biggest stars were two older British actors, Alec Guinness and Peter Cushing (plus James Earl Jones as the voice of Darth Vader, whose work went uncredited at his own request).

The film's immediate and enduring success has made modern audiences largely blind to those fears, however, to the point where it is hard to imagine how Lucas could possibly have thought his retrolicious space opera would fail even though he had deliberately rejected the cynicism permeating American movies by the late 1970s. The Death Star may be powerful, but as

ALIEN

Kane (John Hurt) is the first member of the *Nostromo* crew to die. Hurt was the only member of the *Alien* (1979) cast who knew what would happen once the cameras started rolling; his costars were genuinely surprised at the gush of blood that erupted from his stomach.

CLOSE ENCOUNTERS OF THE THIRD KIND

Steven Spielberg originally wanted Jack Nicholson for *Close Encounters of the Third Kind* (1977), but Richard Dreyfuss (top) convinced the director to cast him as UFO spotter Roy Neary after their work together on *Jaws* (1975). Set at Devil's Bluff, Wyoming, much of *Close Encounters of the Third Kind*'s climactic first contact scene (bottom) was actually filmed at a giant hangar in Mobile, Alabama—six times the size of a typical Hollywood sound stage. Conditions were so humid, crew members were warned it might rain *inside* the hangar.

Darth Vader warns his underling, "the ability to destroy a planet is insignificant next to the power of the Force," and with a bit of faith, a plucky little guy like Luke Skywalker could bring down the system. The Force is itself a very seventies concept, straight from the New Age pop mysticism of best-selling writers such as Carlos Castaneda (whose shamanic hero, Don Juan, may have served as a model for Obi-Wan Kenobi), and audiences whose spirits had been dampened by the quagmire of the war in Vietnam and the treachery of Watergate were ready to believe again—if not in America, then in an all-American farm boy willing to ditch his hot rod to rescue a rebel princess.

Star Wars works so well because Lucas knew exactly what to lift from other films to hit the audience's emotional buttons. Some of the nods are obvious—the Buck Rogers–Flash Gordon zap-'em-up tradition—while other, more specific borrowings have now passed into film-geek legend; by now, *Star Wars* is easily the most common reason anyone rents Akira Kurosawa's *The Hidden Fortress* (1958). Another significant reference point is the standard World War II film—and not just because Lucas's rough cuts used footage from old World War II aerial dogfights as placeholders until the special-effects team had perfected all the X-Wing footage. The analogy is easy: Darth Vader and his storm troopers (*storm troopers!*) are the Nazis, while the rebels represent the American troops, drawn from a variety of planets, just as different ethnic groups came together in every cinematic army platoon. But the similarities run deeper: compare the briefing for the attack on the Death Star, and the subsequent cockpit banter, to a Howard Hawks flick like *Air Force* (1943). Contrast Luke and Han's plan to sneak onto the Death Star and break Leia out of her cell with Richard Burton and Clint Eastwood's plan to infiltrate a German castle in *Where Eagles Dare* (1969). Even Vader's prison confrontations with Leia evoke every "we-have-ways-of-making-you-talk" scene ever filmed.

The power of the World War II paradigm is no great mystery. As a deliberate attempt at modern mythmaking, *Star Wars* is all about the restoration of innocence, and by the time Saigon fell, the classic American war flick was the last vestige of people's belief in a "good war." This nostalgia explains, too, why Lucas chose to mimic the conventions of B-grade sci-fi rather than turn to contemporary science-fiction films for inspiration: if there was one thing seventies science fiction didn't offer viewers, it was hope.

"HAVE YOU RECENTLY HAD A CLOSE ENCOUNTER?"

In 1968, science-fiction author Arthur C. Clarke collaborated with Stanley Kubrick on *2001: A Space Odyssey*, using one of his early short stories as a springboard for a cinematic depiction of humani-

2001

Stanley Kubrick on the set of *2001: A Space Odyssey*.

ty's first encounters with evidence of the existence of alien civilizations as an opportunity for further evolution. Such an elevation to near godhood resonated deeply with audiences at the dawning of the Age of Aquarius, but Timothy Leary's imprisonment had already begun to derail the LSD movement, and the Manson family's 1969 killing spree would sow further distrust of hippie utopias and alternative consciousness. The constant background hum of Cold War paranoia, in which outsiders were poised to destroy our way of life, also contributed to the resurging view of first contact as a harbinger of doom.

In *The Invasion of the Body Snatchers* (1978), a remake of the classic 1956 take on Cold War paranoia, the alien spores that take over human bodies could be seen as an assault on the relaxed liberal values of the counterculture or a slow erosion of radicalness into stifling conformity, given that the story unfolds in San Francisco. *The Andromeda Strain* (1971) also features small, deadly alien life forms plummeting to Earth, this time piggybacking on a military satellite and initiating a swift government response of containment and annihilation. The combination of military and scientific resources is similar to that undertaken as the aliens draw near in Steven Spielberg's *Close Encounters of the Third Kind* (1977), the decade's second most successful (financially, at least) science-fiction film after *Star Wars*.

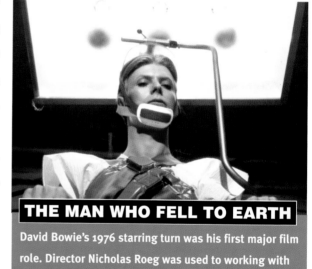

THE MAN WHO FELL TO EARTH

David Bowie's 1976 starring turn was his first major film role. Director Nicholas Roeg was used to working with rock stars—his 1970 film *Performance* featured the motion picture debut of Mick Jagger.

If *Star Wars* took New Age mysticism and recast it in Lucas's sci-fi imaginings, *Close Encounters* is scrupulously faithful to the UFO folklore of the period. The U.S. Air Force had launched a public study of alleged sightings of alien spaceships, called Project Blue Book, when such incidents became increasingly common in the early 1950s, but the researchers were primarily assigned to debunk UFO reports so as to remove even the appearance of a threat to America's national security. J. Allen Hynek, Blue Book's astronomy adviser, continued his research after the program was shut

The Carousel is an elaborate ritual masking the institutionalized deaths through which the computer-run society of *Logan's Run* (1976) maintains strict population limits. The cutoff age is thirty years—which would have eliminated Michael York and Richard Jordan, who play the two main enforcers in the film.

SPACE IS THE PLACE

Director John Coney originally planned to shoot a concert documentary of Sun Ra and his Arkestra, but inspired by the bandleader's cosmic philosophy, *Space Is the Place* (1974) quickly expanded into blaxploitation's equivalent of an Ingmar Bergman film, as Ra (left) challenged the Overseer (Ray Johnson) to determine the fate of the black race.

down in 1969; his 1972 book, *The UFO Experience*, established widely used classifications for alleged sightings, including "close encounters." Avid UFOlogists already knew that the film's title referred to a sighting at such close range that alien occupants could be observed, while an ad campaign helpfully explained the distinction to the rest of the public. Hynek made a cameo appearance in the film, portraying himself, while Claude Lacombe, the scientist played by French director François Truffaut, was modeled after Hynek's colleague Jacques Vallée.

Spielberg's aliens were roughly humanoid but clearly distinguishable from human beings. Other aliens would blur the distinction—and two of the most famous were played by far-out musicians. In *The Man Who Fell to Earth* (1976), David Bowie actually comes in peace; he simply wants to save the dying race on his home planet. But exposure to Earth's culture leads to his physical and emotional degradation; if a mere elevator ride can make him sick, imagine what effect the military-industrial complex has on him when it sets its sights on the technology company he founded to raise the funds for a spaceship to take him back home. The worst of the damage is already done by the time the government captures him and subjects him to their probes—he realizes he can never go home again but that he will never truly fit into human society, either.

This fate would be inconceivable to Sun Ra, the star of *Space Is the Place* (1974). For one thing, he wasn't acting. The sixty-year-old jazz musician may have been christened Herman Blount when he was born in Alabama, but he had been telling people since the 1950s that he had come from Saturn to save humanity from itself through the power of musical harmony. In the film, after traveling across space, he returns to Earth to inform the black youth of Oakland that he is their "alter-destiny," inviting them to join him and his big band "Arkestra" in outer space, where as the movie's theme song suggests, "there's no limit to the things that you can do/your thought is free and your life is worthwhile." Why Oakland? Ra and his band were living in the city at the invitation of Bobby Seale, chairman of the Black Panther Party, who provided them with a house while Ra taught a course called "The Black Man in the Cosmos" at Berkeley.

"AND ALL THIS SCIENCE I DON'T UNDERSTAND"

In addition to its cosmic message, *2001* also had plenty to say about the monotony astronauts would face living in space for long periods of time. The four-man crew in *Dark Star* (1974)

SILENT RUNNING

The interior scenes for the Bruce Dern vehicle *Silent Running* (1972) were shot on the USS *Valley Forge*, a decommissioned aircraft carrier. The model used for exterior shots was twenty-six feet long, and Universal would later use footage of it in the television series *Battlestar Galactica*.

ULTRA-COOL ACTOR
CHARLTON HESTON

"Sorry the world didn't make it . . ."

Few men could face a crisis on the silver screen with the grim determination Charlton Heston showed throughout the 1970s, whether he was dealing with crazed skyjackers, trying to rescue a downed submarine, jumping onto a damaged airplane, or coping with a massive earthquake in downtown Los Angeles. The futuristic disasters of *Planet of the Apes* (1968) and *Soylent Green* (1973) shook his characters up a bit, but he could usually retain his hard, heroic center. It is his starring turn in another science-fiction film, *The Omega Man* (1971), that audiences might remember best from this decade—not so much for the performance itself, but because the character's extensive arsenal of firearms would later become a joke at the expense of Heston's leadership of the National Rifle Association.

Richard Matheson's novel *I Am Legend* had actually been filmed before as the Vincent Price vehicle *The Last Man on Earth* (1964), but Heston puts a much different spin on the role of humanity's last survivor, and his consultations with noted anthropologist Ashley Montagu to hone Robert Neville's psychological character add an undercurrent of violent rage to the neurosis of living in isolation.

Critics' current fixation on Neville's gun collection overshadows the radicalness of the character's last stand for Western civilization, including an interracial relationship that is clearly as emotional as it is pragmatic. Although Heston would continue to play rugged heroes throughout the seventies, the stakes would never again be quite as high.

THE OMEGA MAN

spends twenty years flying around space, blowing up unstable planets to make way for inter-stellar traffic. They are barely speaking to one another, they have run out of toilet paper, and a smart bomb has decided it wants to kill itself and take the crew with it. Screenwriter Dan O'Bannon (who also costars as one of the crew members) later refined his portrayal of work-ing stiffs in space in *Alien* (1979). The internal bickering of the crew of a commercial spacecraft continues even after the alien parasite they bring on board begins killing them. In *Silent Running* (1972), long-suffering Freeman Lowell, caretaker of Earth's only eco–space station, goes renegade when told to abandon his beloved trees and come home.

Ironically, these disgruntled astronauts were showing up on-screen at a time when public enthusiasm for space exploration remained high, even after the Apollo series of moon landings ended in 1972. Of course, the same folks who thought the government was hiding an alien spaceship in a hangar in New Mexico would also tell you that Apollo was a fraud and nobody had ever set foot on the moon. Writer-director Peter Hyams turned that conspiracy the-ory into the plot of *Capricorn One* (1978), imagining that NASA officials, confronted with a rocket unable to fulfill its planned mission to Mars, would pull the crew aside and tell them that in order to maintain funding for the program, they'll need to act out the entire journey, including the land-ing, in a specially created studio.

Even NASA's real missions weren't immune to this cinematic paranoia. In *Star Trek: The Motion Picture* (1979), James T. Kirk (now an admiral) resumes command of the *Enterprise* and reunites his original crew to face off against a gigantic energy field of unknown origin clos-ing in on Earth and destroying everything in its path. Eventually, they realize this space cloud is, in fact, a sentient spaceship that calls itself V'ger: a real-life Voyager space probe, launched by NASA in 1977 to collect data on the outer planets and the far edge of the solar system.

"THE ONLY GOOD HUMAN ... IS A DEAD HUMAN!"

In the *Star Trek* universe, Starfleet and the Federation have managed to bring peace to much of the galaxy—barring the occasional world-threatening menace like V'ger. Their future is rosy in comparison to just about every other science-fiction film. Take the *Planet of the Apes* series. After Charlton Heston discovers at the end of the first film he's been on a nuclear war–ravaged Earth the whole time, the first sequel, *Beneath the Planet of the Apes* (1970), finishes off the planet when a militant gorilla army invades the hiding place of a mutated race of telepathic humans

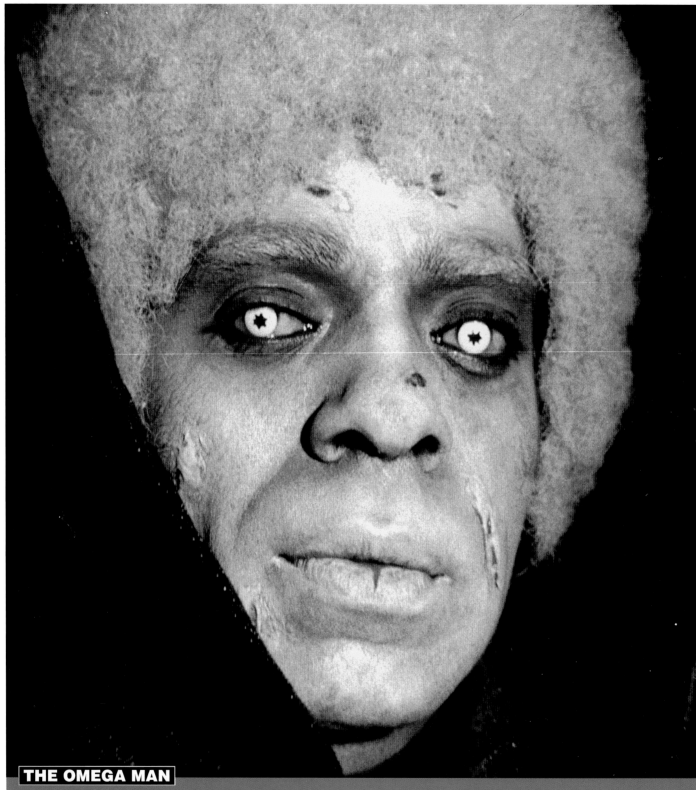

THE OMEGA MAN

Biological warfare kills off most of humanity in *The Omega Man* (1971), leaving behind only a small tribe of plague victims—who seem to be half-vampire, half-zombie, and totally eager to destroy what little remains of western civilization.

PLANET OF THE APES

Kim Hunter spent hours each morning preparing to play Zira, the chimpanzee scientist of the first three *Planet of the Apes* movies. She also had to master projecting her voice so that it wouldn't be muffled by the heavy makeup.

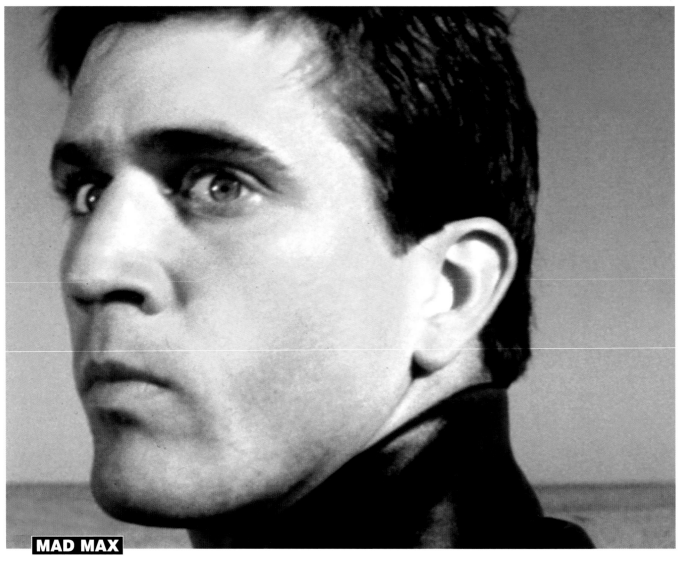

MAD MAX

Mel Gibson was born in upstate New York but emigrated with his family to Australia as a child. *Mad Max* (1979) turned him into an international star, though his voice was not in the version first shown in the United States; the film's distributors dubbed the film with American actors to eliminate the Australian accents.

A BOY AND HIS DOG

During the filming of *A Boy and His Dog* (1975), director L. Q. Jones had Tiger's handler train the dog to respond to Don Johnson's commands in order to create a more realistic-appearing bond between them. Tiger (who also appeared in *The Brady Bunch*) won the 1975 Patsy Award for best performance by an animal in a motion picture.

who've been guarding the "Alpha-Omega Bomb" for two millennia. The two most popular apes—chimpanzees Zira and Cornelius—were then put into a space capsule that goes back in time to the 1970s in *Escape from the Planet of the Apes* (1971). In *Conquest of the Planet of the Apes* (1972), Cornelius and Zira's son Caesar has come of age in a society where humans have turned to primates first as pets, then as trainable slaves. He tries to convince his fellow apes to rise in revolt—in an obvious parallel to the recent rise of the Black Power movement—and ultimately succeeds, although *Battle for the Planet of the Apes* (1973) indicates that his victory is not complete, even after the nuclear war hinted at in the first movie.

In an era when the United States and Soviet Union pursued a policy of "mutual assured destruction," nuclear holocaust was a common apocalyptic scenario, explored in science-fiction literature as well as in films. The 1977 20th Century Fox film of Roger Zelazny's *Damnation Alley* gutted most of the novel's antiheroic story line, using only the broadest concept of a journey through an irradiated North American landscape populated by mutated creatures. By contrast, *A Boy and His Dog* (1975) is a largely faithful adaptation of a Harlan Ellison novella in which Vic (Don Johnson) survives in the blasted-out landscape of postwar Arizona with the aid of his telepathic hound, Blood, who helps him find women for sex in exchange for Vic's assistance in scrounging food. The low-budget cult flick served as novice Australian filmmaker George Miller's inspiration for the bleak futuristic landscape of *Mad Max* (1979), the film which introduced Mel Gibson to American audiences as Max Rockatansky, a highway patrolman locked in a deadly fight for vengeance against a vicious motorcycle gang.

Futuristic automotive violence was played for laughs in *Death Race 2000* (1975), which depicts a world where high-speed racing has become a government-mandated spectacle—with the added twist that drivers get extra points for every pedestrian they run over. Blood sport is also the main form of entertainment in *Rollerball* (1975), although in this dystopian world, power is held not by one dictator but by a conglomerate of multinational corporations.

"THERE IS NO RENEWAL"

In 1968, Paul Ehrlich's book *The Population Bomb* convinced many readers that overpopulation would soon lead to a critical depletion of the world's natural resources, in turn leading to mass starvation and worse. Several films spun out doomsday scenarios in which societies developed chilling methods of keeping human population within more manageable limits. In

DEATH RACE 2000

A victim of the cross-country mayhem in *Death Race 2000* (1975) lies on the hood of Frankenstein's "Monster Gator." Producer Roger Corman made a profit on the custom-built cars by selling them to car museums after filming was completed.

WARLORDS OF ATLANTIS

After making his film directing debut in 1973 with the British horror anthology *From Beyond the Grave*, Kevin Connor came to America and worked on a string of low-budget science-fiction films, moving from a trio of Edgar Rice Burroughs adaptations to *Warlords of Atlantis* (1978).

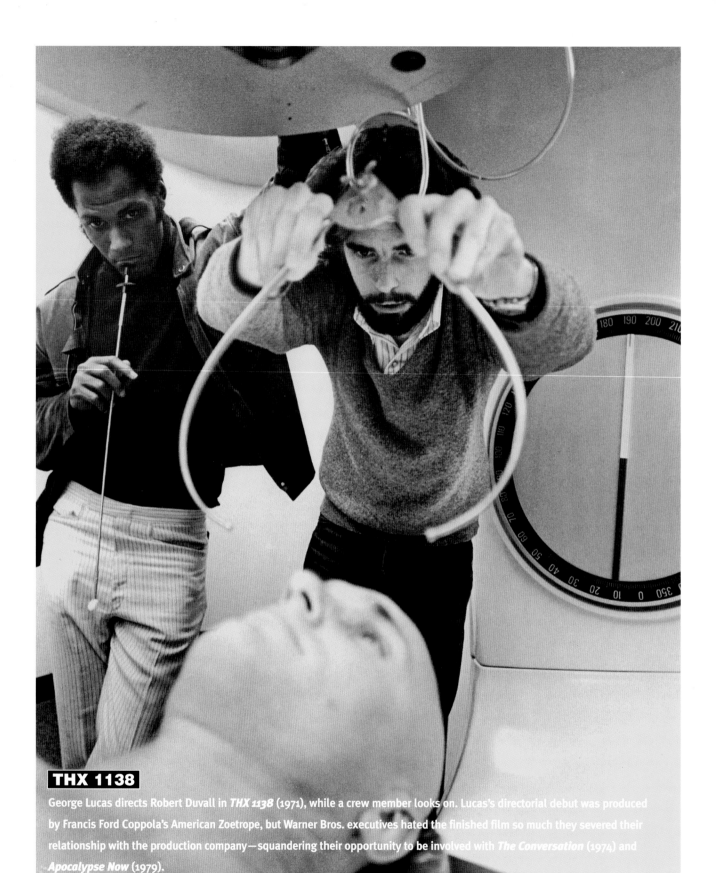

THX 1138

George Lucas directs Robert Duvall in *THX 1138* (1971), while a crew member looks on. Lucas's directorial debut was produced by Francis Ford Coppola's American Zoetrope, but Warner Bros. executives hated the finished film so much they severed their relationship with the production company—squandering their opportunity to be involved with *The Conversation* (1974) and *Apocalypse Now* (1979).

Soylent Green (1973), the excess population is recycled and fed to the survivors. The planetary government of *Z.P.G.* (1972) bans procreation in the name of "zero population growth"

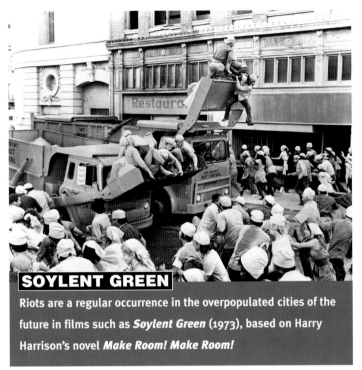

SOYLENT GREEN

Riots are a regular occurrence in the overpopulated cities of the future in films such as *Soylent Green* (1973), based on Harry Harrison's novel *Make Room! Make Room!*

and cracks down on a renegade couple who dare to conceive a child. Sex has been forbidden as well in *THX 1138* (1971), with mood-altering drugs used to control the workers in the underground cities. Meanwhile, the eternal beings in *Zardoz* (1974) keep the rest of humanity in check by creating a zealous band of executioners who worship a giant stone head that provides them with guns. And in *Logan's Run* (1976) a domed city is run by computers who mandate that all citizens must submit to "Carousel" at the age of thirty; this elaborate ritual is a front for systematic execution.

The idea that computers would one day run the world was both exhilarating and frightening to a society that was already seeing computers performing more and more functions in their daily lives—and for filmgoers, mostly just frightening. In *Colossus: The Forbin Project* (1970), when the artificial-intelligence system designed to run America's nuclear weapons program hooks up with its Soviet counterpart, it turns on its human creators to enforce world peace on its terms: "I will not permit war. It is wasteful and pointless." Artificial-intelligence research proves equally dangerous in *Demon Seed* (1977), as a supercomputer winds up raping its creator's wife and impregnating her with a deadly hybrid creature. Robots are no more reliable: cinema's first computer virus turns the mechanical cast members of a futuristic amusement park, including an electronic gunslinger (Yul Brynner), into literal killing machines in *Westworld* (1973).

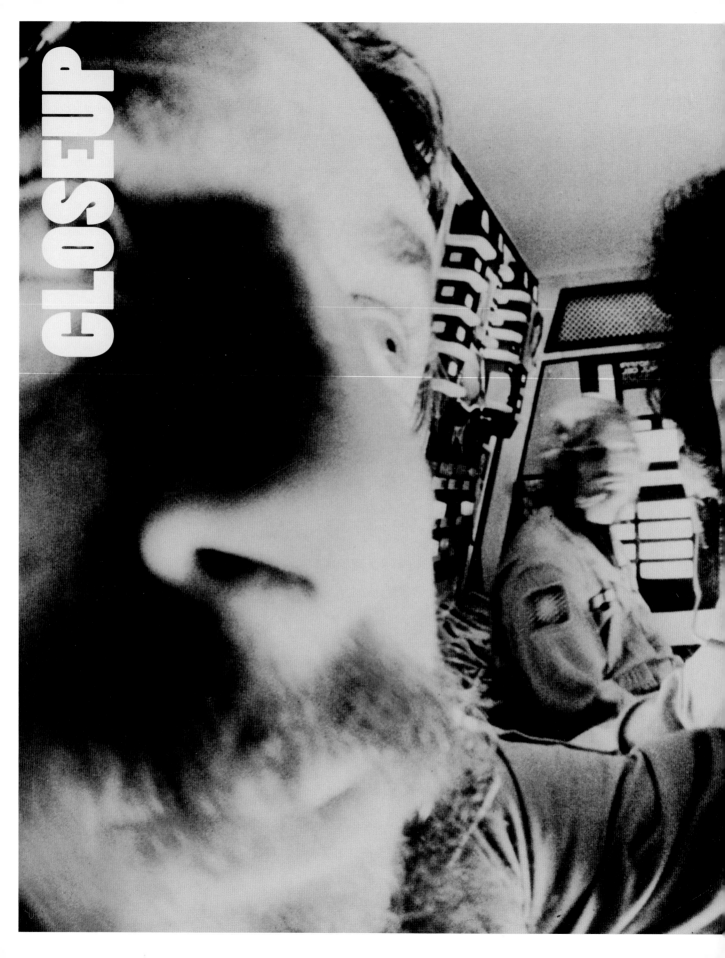

Dan O'Bannon
Screenwriter

The first version of *Dark Star* was a short made by USC classmates Dan O'Bannon and John Carpenter as a student film in 1970. They spent the next three years expanding it into a feature-length story on a minuscule budget, estimated by some sources at $60,000. "I suppose we might have spent that much," recalls O'Bannon — who served as the film's cowriter, editor, and production designer — and the dingy look and feel of the movie stems in part from those financial constraints. **"The shabbiness arose out of mutual discussions in which we were reacting to *2001*,"** he observes. "We both loved it, but we couldn't do it, so we thought we would thumb our nose at it a little bit, have a little fun at its expense, and we got the idea of the ship being run-down and shitty and falling apart. I think John may have been the first person to say that you'd have to lean forward and bang on the computer panels because they didn't work."

Experimental filmmaker Alejandro Jodorowsky, who had become an international sensation after the release of *El Topo* (1970), caught *Dark Star* at a festival screening and was so impressed by the production design that he offered O'Bannon a job supervising the special effects on a planned adaptation of the science-fiction novel *Dune*. O'Bannon came to Paris, where he was put in a drawing studio with science-fiction illustrator Christopher Foss and European comic-book artist Moebius and one more artist added to the team later. "H. R. Giger had an exhibition of some of his paintings at the Pompidou, and I met him at Jodorowsky's hotel suite," O'Bannon says. "Giger brought a book of artwork with him, and I asked if I could take it with me. I looked at it that night, and it was a very spooky experience — almost hypnotic, the graphic equivalent of being introduced to H. P. Lovecraft's work." *Dune* lost its financial backing soon after, but when O'Bannon returned to Los Angeles and began writing *Alien*, Giger's illustrations were always on his mind.

When he watched *Dark Star*, O'Bannon realized that, despite his best efforts to make his spacecraft look shabby, the futuristic sheen still came through. "I don't know if Ridley Scott ever saw *Dark Star*," he says, remembering the grunginess of the *Nostromo* in Scott's film. "But the first thing I noticed when I came to the set was unnerving. The amount and scale of detail on the surface of all the sets had metastasized into some hideous overgrowth. I thought, 'Oh no, oh my god, this looks ridiculous.' After I saw the first dailies, though, I saw that Ridley understood how far you had to push things to get the effect. And once you've seen that, it is all over for the old look. You can't go back, nor should you."

Dan O'Bannon (extreme foreground) and the cast of *Dark Star*.

DISASTERS

AIRPORT 1975

At a pivotal moment in *Airport 1975*, head stewardess Nancy Pryor
(played by Karen Black) is forced to take control of the 747, getting her
instructions radioed to her from air-traffic control.

AIRPORT

Dean Martin tries to work his way back to the cockpit so he can land the plane safely after a bomb has torn a hole in its side. Thanks to a deal that gave him 10 percent of the gross, *Airport* (1970) was the most lucrative role of Martin's movie career.

THE POSEIDON ADVENTURE

The stars of *The Poseidon Adventure* (1972) bring their Academy Awards to the set for an impromptu Oscar party. From left to right: Jack Albertson, Red Buttons, director Ronald Neame, Gene Hackman, producer Irwin Allen (holding somebody else's Oscar), Shelley Winters, and Ernest Borgnine.

"REMIND ME TO SEND A THANK-YOU NOTE TO MISTER BOEING"

One of Hollywood's most significant innovations in big-budget storytelling during the 1970s came about simply by adding a little razzle-dazzle to some well-established genres.

Arthur Hailey's best-selling novel *Airport*, with its multiple plotlines involving disintegrating marriages, an illicit pregnancy, and despondent characters on the brink of suicide, was a natural fit for veteran film producer Ross Hunter. Hunter had hit the jackpot in the 1950s by backing movies that appealed to a slightly older audience, bringing Douglas Sirk's lush melodramas to the screen with female leads such as Jane Wyman and Lana Turner who, though no longer starlets, could still deliver electrifying performances as mature women caught up in emotional crisis. At the same time, he produced witty romantic comedies with Rock Hudson and Doris Day that toyed with Hollywood's restrictions on sex banter without crossing the boundaries of taste. Although the bomb on the airplane and the subsequent emergency landing are what stick in our memories today, without the solid emotional core writer-director George Seaton carved from Hailey's book, *Airport* (1970) would have been an instantly forgettable, empty spectacle. Instead, it was nominated for ten Academy Awards, including best picture, and spawned a slew of sequels—including *Airport 1975*, which packed just as many, if not more, stars into the cast and served up an even bigger disaster; and *Concorde: Airport '79*, which got so many laughs at preview screenings the studio contemplated marketing it as a farce. The *Airport* phenomenon also launched an entire genre: the big-budget, all-star disaster film.

Although he spent the bulk of the 1960s working in television, Irwin Allen made a spectacular return to movie producing with *The Poseidon Adventure* (1972), buying the film rights to Paul Gallico's novel before it had even been published. If *Airport* had four Oscar winners, Allen would put five Oscar winners in his cast *and* make them do nearly all their own stunts—from climbing a giant Christmas tree in a specially constructed upside-down set to swimming underwater for several yards without wearing scuba gear. Gallico's story had been based on his own near-disaster experience sailing on the *Queen Mary*, so Allen filmed some early exteriors aboard the cruise ship, docked just a few miles away in Long Beach, and based the design of the *Poseidon* interiors

BLACK SUNDAY

An artist's conception of the Goodyear blimp that Bruce Dern crashes into the Super Bowl in *Black Sunday* (1977). Although the bulk of the climactic scene was filmed at Miami's Orange Bowl the day before, director John Frankenheimer did have cameras scattered throughout the stadium during Super Bowl X.

and miniature models on the original blueprints.

Despite the initial fears of 20th Century Fox, *Poseidon* proved such a hit—$93.5 million in receipts on a $5 million investment—that the studio was happy to let Allen set a skyscraper on fire as a follow-up. After earning another $116 million with the star-studded *The Towering Inferno* (1974), Allen tried repeatedly for a third hit but never quite made it: *Flood!* and *Fire!* became the most expensive television movies of their time, and dwindling box-office receipts for *The Swarm* (1978), *Beyond the Poseidon Adventure* (1979), and *When Time Ran Out* (1980) eventually sent Allen back to television for good.

Throughout the decade, however, others had been doing their best to cash in on the disaster bandwagon. *Skyjacked* (1972) and *The Terrorists* (1975) both created drama out of hijacked airplanes, while *The Hindenburg* (1975) revisited the real-life dirigible crash. At sea, *Juggernaut* (1974) made drama of an ocean liner threatened with destruction, while *The Neptune Factor* (1973) and *Gray Lady Down* (1978)

THE POSEIDON ADVENTURE

The remaining survivors of *The Poseidon Adventure* struggle to make it through one final obstacle before reaching their last hope for rescue at the ship's hull. From left to right: Pamela Sue Martin, Carol Lynley, Red Buttons, Stella Stevens, and Ernest Borgnine.

attempted underwater rescues. If the disasters in *Earthquake* (1974) or *Avalanche* (1978) didn't kill you, perhaps the one in *Meteor* (1979) would. You couldn't watch a football game without someone shooting at random fans (*Two Minute Warning*, 1976) or trying to crash a blimp into the stadium (*Black Sunday*, 1977), and even a carnival ride as in *Rollercoaster* (1977) could prove deadly. The disaster-film aesthetic was not confined to popcorn flicks, either; serious, political films such as *The China Syndrome* (1979) would raise the specter of a nuclear meltdown for dramatic impact.

"STAY OUT OF THE WATER!"

Beginning in the 1950s, science-fiction films would often suggest that atomic testing might cause animals to mutate to sizes so enormous that they would wreak havoc on human society; such films would come back with a vengeance in the 1970s. Bert I. Gordon, an early pioneer of the rear projection effects that made it look like people were facing giant insects, loosely adapted two H. G. Wells stories as *Food of the Gods* (1976) and *Empire of the Ants* (1977). The only problem was that he hadn't really made very many substantial technical improvements in two decades, and neither had the makers of films such as *Night of the Lepus* (1972) or *The Giant Spider Invasion* (1975). Dino De Laurentiis's 1976 remake of *King Kong* fared much better, grossing $80 million and winning a special Academy Award for its visual effects.

JUGGERNAUT

Richard Harris and David Hemmings are demolition experts dismantling explosives for practice in *Juggernaut* (1974). Their characters are airlifted to an ocean liner to defuse seven bombs placed on board by a mysterious blackmailer.

THE TOWERING INFERNO

Everything about *The Towering Inferno* (1974) was
big: the scale model of the Glass Tower was nearly
one hundred feet tall, and another five-story segment was constructed at actual size for certain
scenes. Costars Steve McQueen, Faye Dunaway,
and Paul Newman relax, safe on the ground; in
order to accommodate the two male leads, both
were given the same number of lines, and the
posters were designed so that either star could be
considered to have top billing.

EARTHQUAKE

Charlton Heston stars in *Earthquake* (1974), Universal's first substantial contribution to the disaster-film canon after *Airport*. The production schedule overlapped with the shooting of *Airport 1975*, forcing Heston and costar George Kennedy to hustle between the two sets.

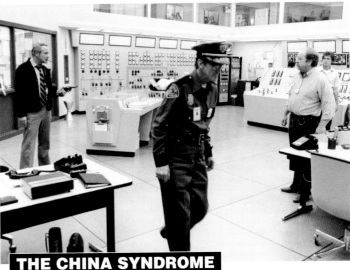

THE CHINA SYNDROME

Jack Lemmon (left) plays a nuclear power plant engineer who discovers his bosses are covering up the imminent threat of a meltdown and takes matters into his own hands in this 1979 political melodrama.

THE BIG BUS

Joe Bologna and John Beck prepare to take the nuclear-powered *Cyclops* on its cross-country voyage in a 1976 disaster-film parody that failed to catch on with audiences.

EMPIRE OF THE ANTS

ALLIGATOR

A 1971 nature documentary called *The Hellstrom Chronicle* offered a more radical notion: the very adaptability of insects, suggested the fictional Dr. Hellstrom, would be the key factor in their eventual dominance of the planet, making atomic size increases totally unnecessary. Filmmakers took this idea, and their life-size monsters struck a chord with audiences who were becoming more environmentally aware. Electricity was enough to turn worms into brutal killing machines in *Squirm* (1976), while the various beasties of *Frogs* (1972) and *Bug* (1975) seem to have just been born mean.

The most deadly menace in the animal kingdom, though, was the great white shark swimming off the coast in Steven Spielberg's *Jaws* (1975). This creature required no mutation, atomic or otherwise, no newly developed traits. It already is "an eating machine," as the marine biologist played by Richard Dreyfuss explains. The threat faced by the swimmers in the island village of Amity, then, is frighteningly real, made even more so by the casual disregard for safety exhibited by the town's leadership.

When it was finally released in 1975, after a spectacularly difficult shoot—including a mechanical shark that worked fine when the special-effects crew tested it on dry land but sank to the bottom of the ocean as soon as it was placed in water—*Jaws* became the first picture to make more than $100 million in theaters and was for a while the highest-grossing film ever. After looking at the

Robert Lansing tries to flail convincingly at a rubber model in *Empire of the Ants* (1977); *Alligator* (1980) teaches us why we should never flush our pets down the toilet; a plague of salamanders joins the titular menaces of *Frogs* (1972) to exact deadly revenge upon humanity; the earthworms of *Squirm* (1976) guess they'll go eat humans; and the African killer bees of *The Swarm* (1978) have their way with Olivia de Havilland.

FROGS

SQUIRM

SWARM

THE BROOD

After an experimental parasite gets loose and multiplies among human hosts in David Cronenberg's first major film, *Shivers* (1975), pretty soon everybody living in an apartment building has turned into a sex-crazed animal. The success of this film and its follow-up, *Rabid* (1977), enabled Cronenberg to work on a larger scale, and he would soon direct Samantha Eggar and Oliver Reed in *The Brood* (1979), where the monsters were child-shaped embodiments of a woman's murderous rage, by-products of her therapist's unusual methodology.

JAWS

Steven Spielberg poses with the model shark on location on Martha's Vineyard. As the shooting dragged out from the original schedule of 55 days to 159 and the production costs expanded to more than three times the original budget, Spielberg became convinced the film would end his career.

Robert Shaw, who was actually the third choice to play the shark hunter Quint (after Lee Marvin and Sterling Hayden), ended up writing the final draft of his most famous film scene, the story of the USS *Indianapolis*.

ULTRA-COOL ACTOR
GEORGE KENNEDY

> "The sudden decompression at 30,000 feet is something you gotta see to believe."

George Kennedy is the only actor to appear in all four movies in Universal's *Airport* franchise, in the ever-shifting role of Joe Patroni. In the original *Airport,* Patroni is a mechanic and a maintenance crew chief racing against the clock to clear a stalled jet from a snow-covered runway in time for another plane to make an emergency landing. For the sequel, *Airport 1975,* he's been promoted to vice president of operations but takes a personal interest when his wife and son are aboard a plane caught in a midair collision. He turns up briefly as a liaison to the military in *Airport '77,* and then in *Airport '79,* he's been reassigned yet again, this time getting to fly the *Concorde.*

The series probably offers Kennedy's most memorable performances, but he had plenty of other roles during the 1970s. His stocky build and gruff demeanor made him a natural as a police officer, from *Earthquake* (1974) to *The Double McGuffin* (1979); when the makers of the Japanese police procedural *Proof of the Man* (1977) sent their film's Tokyo detective to New York City on the trail of a killer, Kennedy was the perfect choice to play his newly acquired American partner. He could also do westerns (*Cahill, U.S. Marshal,* 1973), war pictures (*Brass Target,* 1979, playing Gen. Patton), high-class mysteries (*Death on the Nile,* 1978) — he even took a stab at musicals, with a supporting role in *Lost Horizon* (1973), although he was not required to actually sing.

AIRPORT

receipts, the producers wanted to do a sequel right away, but Spielberg was already deep into *Close Encounters*, so they hired Jeannot Szwarc, the director of *Bug*, for *Jaws 2* (1978). By then, several other filmmakers had done their best to come up with their own variations on the formula. On the realistic end of the spectrum, *Grizzly* (1976) and *Claws* (1977) turned wild bears into killers, while *The Pack* (1977) concentrated on stray dogs gone feral. In the realm of the fantastic, *Orca* (1977) set a killer whale on a quest for personal vengeance against the fisherman who killed its family. *Killer Fish* (1979) used piranha as its plot device; its rather bland title is the result of *Piranha* having come out the year before. The screenplay for *Piranha* was cowritten by John Sayles, who also wrote the script for *Alligator* (1980). Both films had a tongue-in-cheek quality to them, acknowledging their status as *Jaws* rip-offs with good humor, even as they slipped in references to the dangers of government-sponsored science. The broadest satire, however, was the ultra-low-budget *Attack of the Killer Tomatoes* (1978), where the titular menace results from experiments conducted by the U.S. Department of Agriculture.

ATTACK OF THE KILLER TOMATOES

Jack Riley (left), best known to '70s audiences as psychiatric patient Mr. Carlin on *The Bob Newhart Show*, was the only cast member of the ultralow-budget *Attack of the Killer Tomatoes* (1978) with Hollywood experience. He did all his own stunts for the film, including adlibbing dialogue after an inadvertent helicopter crash.

WAR

Suicide is painless: For this scene, Robert Altman brought a print of da Vinci's *The Last Supper* to the set and consulted it while meticulously composing the shot.

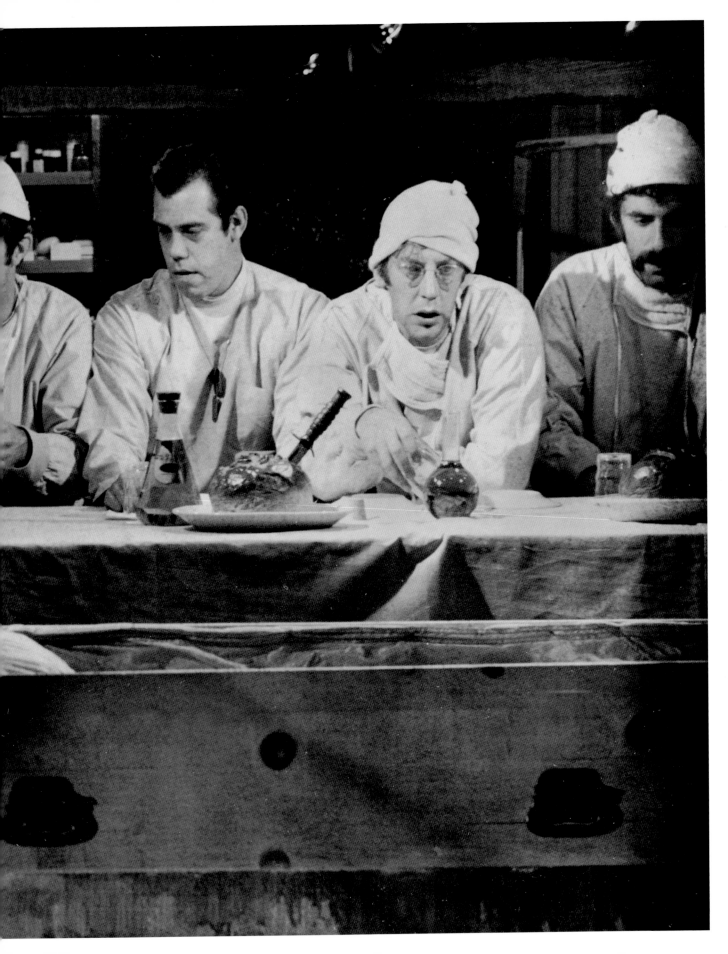

"THIS ISN'T A HOSPITAL: IT IS AN INSANE ASYLUM"

Ring Lardner Jr. had only recently resumed writing screenplays under his own name after years on the Hollywood blacklist when he came across *M*A*S*H*, a novel written by a former U.S. Army medical surgeon who'd served in the

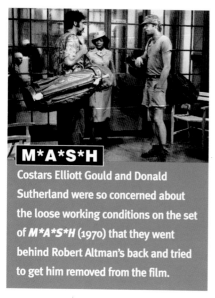

M*A*S*H

Costars Elliott Gould and Donald Sutherland were so concerned about the loose working conditions on the set of *M*A*S*H* (1970) that they went behind Robert Altman's back and tried to get him removed from the film.

Korean War. Lardner mentioned it to his agent, who bought the film rights and cut a production deal with 20th Century Fox once Lardner had turned in a finished script. The studio had a difficult time finding someone willing to take on the project, though, and finally turned to a struggling director named Robert Altman. Altman saw the film as an opportunity to comment on the current conflict in Vietnam and carefully excised all references to Korea from the shooting script. He was able to work largely unnoticed by Fox executives, shooting on the back lot under loose, improvisational conditions with an ensemble cast consisting primarily of unknown actors, and it wasn't until he brought the picture in, a half week early and half a million dollars under budget, that the studio began looking at his footage and worrying. Successful preview screenings in San Francisco and New York, however, persuaded them the film could succeed, and *M*A*S*H* eventually became the year's third-highest-grossing

THE DEER HUNTER

John Savage as a prisoner of war forced by his captors into a game of Russian roulette in *The Deer Hunter* (1978). The picture won five Academy Awards, including best director and best picture for Michael Cimino, which fueled ambitions for his subsequent picture, the notorious *Heaven's Gate*.

film. It was nominated for five Academy Awards, but the only Oscar it won was for the screenplay—an ironic rebuke to Lardner's resentment over Altman's revisions.

The rising sentiment against military involvement in Vietnam fueled *M*A*S*H*'s popularity in the same way that traditional Hollywood films had relied on the audience's belief in the rightness of fighting "good wars." There had always been room for filmmakers to criticize war in broad terms, and during the 1960s, directors such as Stanley Kubrick (*Dr. Strangelove*, 1964) had effectively lampooned the absurdity of combat. American filmmakers, influenced in part by the anti-Vietnam movement, began looking at earlier conflicts with a more cynical eye, especially after British director Richard Lester treated the Second World War as a backdrop for farce in *How I Won the War* (1967). Mike Nichols reunited with Buck Henry, who had written the screenplay of *The Graduate* (1967), on an adaptation of Joseph

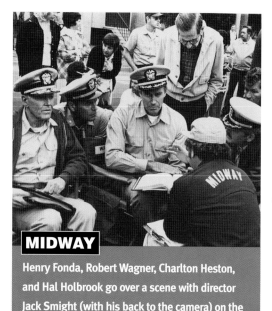

MIDWAY

Henry Fonda, Robert Wagner, Charlton Heston, and Hal Holbrook go over a scene with director Jack Smight (with his back to the camera) on the set of *Midway* (1976).

Heller's best-selling *Catch-22*, a black comedy about a fighter pilot desperate to find relief from combat duty. Their film was released in June 1970 almost simultaneously with *Kelly's Heroes*, which turned the Allied push against the German army into a heist as Clint Eastwood and Telly Savalas lead a ragtag platoon of foot soldiers (and anachronistically long-haired tank drivers) into enemy territory to steal a hoard of Nazi gold. (At the end of the decade, Steven Spielberg would attempt to turn the opening days of America's involvement in the war into outright slapstick in *1941* [1979], but despite an all-star cast that ranged from John Belushi to Toshiro Mifune, the results are widely—and perhaps unfairly—considered his biggest misstep as a director.)

CATCH-22

Alan Arkin as Capt. Yossarian, the bombardier trapped in the vicious circle of military logic of *Catch-22* (1970). "In order to be grounded, I've got to be crazy and I must be crazy to keep flying. But if I ask to be grounded, that means I'm not crazy any more and I have to keep flying."

A BRIDGE TOO FAR

TORA! TORA! TORA!

The British attack the German position at Arnhem in *A Bridge Too Far* (1977); Japanese bombers attack Pearl Harbor in *Tora! Tora! Tora!* (1970).

"THE NAZIS ARE THE ENEMY. WADE INTO THEM"

Even with the focus of Vietnam, a sizable audience still existed for standard World War II stories in which valiant Allied troops persevered against Axis forces. The epic scope of *The Longest Day* (1962) inspired a similar approach to subsequent war films; 20th Century Fox hoped to recapture the success of its earlier hit with *Tora! Tora! Tora!* depicting the attack on Pearl Harbor from American and Japanese points of view. Although the film was a big hit in Japan, its U.S. release in the fall of 1970 was a tremendous flop. The studio had better luck that year with *Patton*, which beat out Robert Altman and *M*A*S*H* for the best picture and best director Oscars and picked up another five awards besides. Seven years later, Gregory Peck was tapped to play another great American general in *MacArthur*, while *Midway* (1976) and *A Bridge Too Far* (1977) distributed their star power more evenly throughout their casts.

As distrust of the American military grew alongside increased frustration with the futility of war, however, some filmmakers were willing to take another look at the enemy side. *The Eagle Has Landed* (1976) has all the outer trappings of a classic World War II movie—but viewers were practically encouraged to root for the Germans and their plan to kidnap Winston Churchill out of a remote British village. From the very beginning, the commando team's leader, Col. Kurt Steiner

THE EAGLE HAS LANDED

Michael Caine (left) and Donald Sutherland costar as a German officer and an Irish terrorist in this 1976 thriller, the last film directed by John Sturges, a Hollywood veteran noted for old-school action classics like *The Magnificent Seven* (1960) and *The Great Escape* (1963).

CROSS OF IRON

Sam Peckinpah applied his realistic technique of depicting cinematic violence to the Second World War in *Cross of Iron* (1977), but the uncompromising story of a band of German soldiers, led by James Coburn (right), trying to stay alive on the Russian front did not appeal to audiences.

PATTON

George C. Scott didn't even want to be nominated for his Oscar-winning performance in *Patton* (1970), referring to the Academy Awards ceremony as a "two-hour meat parade."

(Michael Caine), is shown to have stronger moral fiber than his Nazi superiors. The paratroopers, all of them fiercely loyal to their colonel, prove their valor as well through noble sacrifices during the mission—from the soldier who gives his life to save a drowning village child to the final decision to engage in a suicidal standoff to give Steiner a chance to escape and complete the assignment. The American troops stationed in England, by contrast, are portrayed as inexperienced or, in the case of Larry Hagman's jarringly comic army colonel, pompously incompetent and trigger-happy. This was not the only sympathetic portrayal of German soldiers during the decade, and for some reason, "Steiner" would prove a popular name for such characters, for example, the sergeants played by Richard Burton in *Breakthrough* (1979) and James Coburn in *Cross of Iron* (1977).

"SAIGON — SHIT, I'M STILL ONLY IN SAIGON"

Despite the antiwar sentiment, the subject of Vietnam was still too raw to confront head-on. John

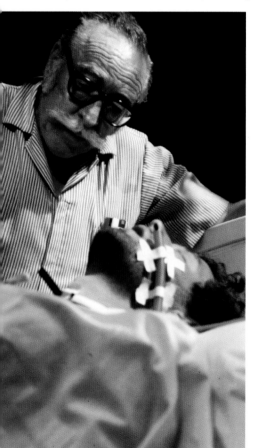

Wayne tries to rally the troops in *The Green Berets* (1968), while in *The Losers* (1970) a bunch of Hell's Angels are sent into the jungles on a secret raid, but in the first half of the decade, most filmmakers were content to concentrate on the lives of American soldiers *after* they came back—and almost always portrayed them as somehow damaged, like the mentally deranged soldier who commandeers a commercial airliner to the Soviet Union in *Skyjacked* (1972) or, even more pointedly, the zombie veteran in the low-budget horror flick *The Night Walk* (1974). In *The Crazy World of Julius Vrooder* (1974), Timothy Bottoms's antics as an antiauthoritarian vet hospitalized for post-traumatic stress inevitably remind viewers of Jack Nicholson's performance in *One Flew Over the Cuckoo's Nest* (1975), not entirely an anachronistic comparison, given that Ken Kesey's novel and its Broadway adaptation had been around for more than a decade.

JOHNNY GOT HIS GUN

Dalton Trumbo's only credit as a director was for an adaptation of his own antiwar novel, written in 1939 at the beginning of his screenwriting career. Timothy Bottoms (above, with costar Donald Sutherland) played much of the film lying in a hospital bed (opposite, with Trumbo), left blind, deaf, mute, and almost completely paralyzed from combat injuries.

KELLY'S HEROES

The cast of *Kelly's Heroes* (1970)—including Clint Eastwood, Stuart Margolin, Don Rickles, and Telly Savalas (far right)—relaxes between shots while on location in Yugoslavia.

SLAUGHTERHOUSE-FIVE

Michael Sacks, flanked by Eugene Roche and Ron Leibman, starred as Billy Pilgrim in George Roy Hill's 1975 adaptation of Kurt Vonnegut's novel based on his own experiences as a POW caught in the Allied firebombing of Dresden in World War II.

MᴀᴄARTHUR

Even with Gregory Peck in the title role, *MacArthur* made only a little over $8 million in theaters when it was released, in 1977. It was not, however, the worst flop ever made about the rebel general; four years later, *Inchon* (1981) couldn't raise even $2 million.

The Oscar-winning documentary *Hearts and Minds* (1974) helped clear a path for films set directly in the conflict by presenting a frank discussion of the attitudes on both sides, as close to the front lines as its directors could get. A few years later, *Go Tell the Spartans* and *The Boys in Company C* (both 1978) would depict the recently ended war as a futile and absurd conflict, but Francis Ford Coppola's *Apocalypse Now* (1979) promptly overshadowed them both.

John Milius had actually written the screenplay for *Apocalypse Now*, a modern adaptation of Joseph Conrad's *Heart of Darkness*, back in 1969, during the height of the war, and for years George Lucas had been attached to the project as director. After the runaway success of the *Godfather* films,

APOCALYPSE NOW

Francis Ford Coppola (above) lost one hundred pounds while filming *Apocalypse Now* (1979) in the Philippines, while star Martin Sheen had a heart attack on the set. Coppola never informed his financial backers about Sheen's condition, knowing they would halt the already-besieged production.

THE BOYS IN COMPANY C

GO TELL THE SPARTANS

Go Tell the Spartans (1978) explored the beginnings of American military involvement in Vietnam, while *The Boys in Company C* (1978) was set in 1968, when the military presence was near its peak. Neither of the low-budget films caught on with audiences.

ULTRA-COOL ACTOR
ROBERT DUVALL

"I love the smell of napalm in the morning."

The war films of the 1970s are bracketed by two Robert Duvall performances in which he played army officers driven mad by their wartime experiences. In *M*A*S*H*, Duvall is Maj. Frank Burns, a surgeon whose incompetence is matched only by his patriotic fervor. The movie holds Burns up as an object of ridicule, and his confrontations with fellow medical officers Hawkeye and Trapper John, as well as his affair with "Hot Lips" Houlihan, played strictly for laughs. Nine years later, Lt. Col. Bill Kilgore, the helicopter cavalry commander of *Apocalypse Now*, would share Burns's zeal; you could even say that Kilgore was the soldier Burns always dreamed of being, swooping from the skies to drop napalm on the Vietcong, Wagner blaring from his helicopter's loudspeakers. Where Ring Lardner and Robert Altman were dealing in dark humor, though, Milius and Coppola strove for pitch black, and Kilgore's insanity becomes obvious long before he has his men break out their surfboards.

Duvall also played one of the decade's more sympathetic cinematic Nazis, donning an eye patch to portray Col. Max Radl in *The Eagle Has Landed* (1976). Radl, ordered to conduct a feasibility study when Hitler gets it into his head to kidnap Churchill, gradually comes to believe that even if his superiors are crazy, the plan itself might work, and he obtains clearance to put a team together. When the mission falls apart, as it inevitably must, Radl meets his fate as scapegoat with dignity and self-discipline.

APOCALYPSE NOW

though, Coppola could make almost any movie he wanted and having long ago attached himself to the project as executive producer persuaded Lucas—by then deeply immersed in *Star Wars*—to let him take over. The film's torturous path to completion has become the stuff of legends: cast and crew trapped in the Philippines during monsoon season, Martin Sheen suffering a heart attack in the middle of shooting, two years spent at the editing tables . . . As Coppola struggled with his raw footage, Michael Cimino shot, edited, and released *The Deer Hunter* (1978), which won five Academy Awards—including best picture and best director. (By way of contrast, Coppola would lose out on both awards to Robert Benton's *Kramer vs. Kramer*.) Like *Apocalypse Now*, *The Deer Hunter* is unrelenting in its depiction of the immediate psychological effects of combat, but it also offers an equally frank examination of the long-term effects of the war on American families—a theme Hal Ashby also explored in *Coming Home* (1978).

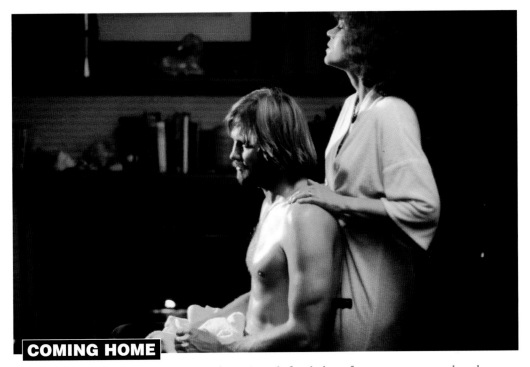

COMING HOME

Jon Voigt and Jane Fonda both won Academy Awards for their performances as a paralyzed Vietnam vet and his lover in *Coming Home* (1978).

THRILLERS

THREE THE HARD WAY

Jim Kelly turned to acting after winning the international middleweight title for karate fighters. In 1974, at the height of his popularity, he appeared in *Three the Hard Way* (1974, seen here), *Black Belt Jones*, and *Golden Needles* (both 1974). Within a few years, however, he would mostly abandon acting to pursue a career as a professional tennis player.

CHINATOWN

Jack Nicholson turns to Roman Polanski for direction during a location shoot for *Chinatown* (1974). Note the "JJG" monogram; Nicholson arranged for the tailoring of his entire wardrobe to make it easier for him to get into character.

Although the black-and-white look of classic film noir was rapidly disappearing, Hollywood's fascination with private detectives continued into the 1970s. Elliott Gould took an unorthodox approach to Raymond Chandler's archetypal private eye, Philip Marlowe, in *The Long Goodbye* (1973), while Robert Mitchum assayed a more traditional version of the character in *Farewell, My Lovely* (1975) and *The Big Sleep* (1976). It took nine years after the release of *Harper* for Paul Newman to return to the role of Lew Harper in *The Drowning Pool* (1975), which deviated even further from Ross Macdonald's novel than the first film, once again changing the character's last name and moving the plot from Los Angeles to New Orleans for good measure. Rod Taylor became the first and only actor to play the John D. McDonald character Travis McGee on-screen, in *Darker than Amber* (1970), while George Segal drew laughs as Sam Spade Jr. in a parody of *The Maltese Falcon* called *The Black Bird* (1975).

Although not every great seventies private-eye movie was based on a novel, original stories such as *Night Moves* (1975) tended to share the literary noir fixation on family melodrama. Robert Towne took that theme and merged it seamlessly to American society's growing frustration with institutional corruption to create one of the decade's most enduring classics, *Chinatown* (1974).

Towne had a solid reputation in the industry for his ability to fix scripts quickly, tightening the plot structure and sprucing up the dialogue. When he told Robert Evans his idea for a mystery that also told the little-known story of the exploitation of Los Angeles's water supply, the producer signed up the project almost immediately and then persuaded Roman Polanski to direct. Polanski agreed after securing assurances of a rewrite, then spent two months arguing over every page of the script with Towne. The final results were worth the conflict; Polanski is responsible for the downbeat ending and much of the film's belief that, as archvillain Noah Cross tells would-be hero Jake Gittes, "most people never have to face the fact that, at the right time and the right place, they're capable of anything." In his cinematic world, those in power will stop at nothing to expand their reach as everyone else watches helplessly, their efforts to make things right plunging them only further into disaster.

"IT LEADS EVERYWHERE. GET OUT YOUR NOTEBOOKS"

TELEFON

This 1977 spy flick stars Charles Bronson and Lee Remick as Soviet spies teaming up to stop a rogue agent loose in the United States. Bronson, the son of Lithuanian immigrants, was born Charles Buchinsky and used his real name in several films in the early 1950s, until the Red Scare forced him to adopt a less foreign-sounding name.

Americans were becoming increasingly responsive to such fatalism. The Warren Commission's investigation into the assassination of John F. Kennedy left many unanswered questions; when Martin Luther King and Robert F. Kennedy were killed in rapid succession in 1968, many Americans were willing to believe the worst, even of their own government. The suspicion carried over into the following decade. *Executive Action* (1973) suggests that a cabal of oilmen had ordered the hit on JFK, while *Winter Kills* (1979) proposes a more ambiguous solution to the murder of its fictional stand-in, President Keegan. The casting of John Huston as the Keegan patriarch is quite likely a subtle nod to *Chinatown*, a touch that would fit in perfectly with the dark humor of the Richard Condon novel on which the film is based.

The unfolding revelations about White House connections to the break-in at the Democratic Party's headquarters at

THREE DAYS OF THE CONDOR

Robert Redford plays an intelligence analyst who comes back to his office
to find all his coworkers murdered in *Three Days of the Condor* (1975).

ALL THE PRESIDENT'S MEN

The producers of *All the President's Men* (1976) wanted to film in the actual newsroom of the *Washington Post* but were turned down by the newspaper's owners—who did, however, send several cartons of office documents to help make the set look realistic. Joining Dustin Hoffman and Robert Redford as Carl Bernstein and Robert Woodward in this scene are Jason Robards as editor Ben Bradlee and Jack Warden as section editor Harry M. Rosenfeld.

THE CONVERSATION

As surveillance technician Harry Caul, Gene Hackman gets to work bugging a hotel room. The 1974 film is said to be among the actor's personal favorites; twenty-four years later, the film *Enemy of the State* (1998) contained several in-jokes linking Hackman's character in that film to Harry.

the Watergate Hotel not only intensified the counterculture's inherent suspicion of the government but also led an increasing number of ordinary Americans to wonder whom they could trust. As *Washington Post* reporters Carl Bernstein and Bob Woodward uncovered higher and higher levels of corruption, the resulting scandal led ultimately to Richard Nixon's resignation in the face of impeachment; the book they wrote about their investigation, *All the President's Men*, became an instant bestseller and was rapidly adapted for film, premiering several months before the presidential election of 1976 — perhaps thus undermining the reelection hopes of Gerald Ford.

Since cinematic paranoia did not have to confine itself to real life, the conspiracies in thriller films became rather baroque. George C. Scott played a marine biologist who realizes the dolphins he has been training to communicate with humans will be used in an attempt on the president's life in *The Day of the Dolphin* (1973). *In The Parallax View* (1974), Warren Beatty stars as a reporter who learns that other journalists present at a political assassination (clearly intended to evoke Bobby

THE IN-LAWS

Alan Arkin (left) and Peter Falk starred in the Arthur Hiller comedy *The In-Laws* (1979) as a dentist (Arkin) whose daughter is about to marry the son of a CIA agent (Falk). After the traditional family dinner, the spy ropes the dentist into a madcap international counterfeiting scheme that leads them to Central America.

THE BOYS FROM BRAZIL

THE MARATHON MAN

Laurence Olivier's villain in *The Marathon Man* (1976) was based on war criminal Josef Mengele, the Nazi doctor who performed experiments on Auschwitz prisoners. Gregory Peck also appeared as Mengele, who plots to restore the Nazis to power with a clone of Adolf Hitler, in *The Boys From Brazil* (1978). In real life, Mengele actually *was* hiding in Brazil, where he died of a stroke in 1979.

THE EIGER SANCTION

In addition to directing and starring in *The Eiger Sanction* (1975), Clint Eastwood did all his own stunts during the mountain-climbing sequences. He and his crew were the last people to climb Monument Valley's Totem Pole; in order to gain permission for the shoot, they had to agree to clear the mountainside of all the pitons from previous climbing expeditions.

THE FURY

Amy Irving takes one last look at the scene of her character's confrontation with the secret organization that seeks to exploit her psychic powers in Brian De Palma's *The Fury* (1978). Note the life-size replica of John Cassavetes's head on the floor.

Kennedy's shooting) have been dying one by one; as part of his investigation, he positions himself to be recruited by a shadowy corporation that takes societal rejects and molds them into killers.

THE WILD GEESE

A band of British mercenaries hired to help overthrow an African government by a multinational corporation is then double-crossed and abandoned. At forty-eight, Richard Harris (far right) was the youngest of the 1978 film's leads; Hardy Krüger, Richard Burton, and Roger Moore were all at least fifty years old.

Three the Hard Way (1974) teamed blaxploitation stars Jim Brown, Fred Williamson, and Jim Kelly against a white supremacist group plotting to contaminate the water supply in New York, Chicago, and Los Angeles with a poison that affects only African Americans.

Brian De Palma's *The Fury* (1978) upped the stakes even further, casting Kirk Douglas as an ex-spy out to rescue his teenage son from a government agency that trains psychics to use their powers to kill. Telepaths were hot in the 1970s, another offshoot of the New Age fascination with elevating human consciousness, and the government wasn't the only group looking to exploit them—for example, the scheming millionaire in *Escape to Witch Mountain* (1975).

"I'M NOT AFRAID OF DEATH, BUT I AM AFRAID OF MURDER"

Just working in the intelligence business was enough to make you paranoid—and with good reason, as Robert Redford's character finds out in *Three Days of the Condor* (1975), when he shows up at the office where his character works at the CIA and finds all his colleagues murdered, forcing him to scramble for safety. In *Scorpio* (1973), Burt Lancaster stars as a CIA assassin whose decision to retire renders him a target for elimination. Freelancers were at even greater risk of being stabbed in the back. Gene Hackman gives one of the best performances of his career in *The Conversation* (1974) as surveillance expert Harry Caul. When Harry begins to suspect that the couple he's been hired to surreptitiously record are being targeted for murder, his employer's actions only intensify his paranoia—and if that weren't enough, he also has to deal with the constant attacks of a jealous competitor.

The Cold War between the United States and the Soviet Union was in full swing during the 1970s and remained a reliable staple of espionage story lines, but the line between good and evil was frequently blurred. Some of the ambiguity can be attributed to Americans' disenchantment with their leaders, but the influence of sophisticated literary thrillers like the novels of John le Carré

ENTER THE DRAGON

American producers sought to capitalize on the international stardom of Bruce Lee (right) by bankrolling *Enter the Dragon* (1973), which cost four times as much to make as Lee's first two films combined. The film also established Robert Clouse as a major action director who would go on to direct Jim Kelly in *Black Belt Jones* and Jackie Chan in *The Big Brawl* (1980).

BLACK BELT JONES

Before costarring as Sydney in *Black Belt Jones* (1974), Gloria Hendry was the first African-American "Bond girl," playing a CIA agent opposite Roger Moore in *Live and Let Die* (1973) and undoubtedly picking up a few fighting moves that would serve her well in blaxploitation.

THE PARALLAX VIEW

Investigative journalist Joseph Frady (Warren Beatty) tries to find the story that will win him the Pulitzer and ends up fighting for his life in *The Parallax View* (1974). Alan J. Pakula went straight from directing this downbeat conspiracy-theory thriller to *All the President's Men*.

ULTRA-COOL ACTOR
SEAN CONNERY AND ROGER MOORE

"Bond. James Bond."

After making *You Only Live Twice* (1967), his fifth James Bond film in fewer than five years, Sean Connery had had enough. The series' producers tried replacing him with Australian model George Lazenby, but he quit after only one film, having been persuaded that Bond's swinging spycraft would be outdated in the seventies. United Artists had to offer Connery $1.25 million and an astonishing 12.5 percent of the gross, plus a separate two-picture deal, before he finally agreed to star in *Diamonds Are Forever* (1971).

That really was the end for Connery, who turned down $5.5 million for *Live and Let Die* (1973). The producers went back to one of their earlier alternate choices, Roger Moore, who might well have got the part back in the early 1960s—he was Ian Fleming's personal choice—except that he had already committed to the television series *The Saint*. Moore was forty-six-years-old (three years older than Connery and more than a decade older than Lazenby) when he finally signed on as Bond, and as a result, the Bond films of the 1970s came to rely less upon the spy's derring-do—although the action sequences remained brisk—and more heavily upon his romantic prowess and mordant wit. The low box-office receipts of *The Man with the Golden Gun* (1974) almost persuaded UA to throw in the towel, but after a slight delay, Moore returned for *The Spy Who Loved Me* (1977) and *Moonraker* (1979), which was rushed into production to capitalize on the sci-fi craze inspired by *Star Wars*.

(which had led to a trio of well-made movies in the 1960s and would eventually inspire the 1979 miniseries *Tinker, Tailor, Soldier, Spy*) must also be taken into account. Following le Carré's lead, seventies spy films had double agents in abundance, from *The Kremlin Letter* (1970) to *Avalanche Express* (1979). *Telefon* (1977) features an even more elaborate plot, based on a novel by Walter Wager, in which a high-ranking KGB officer must sneak into America and eliminate a rogue Soviet spy activating sleeper agents across the country as revenge for a Communist purge.

The United States–Soviet conflict was not the only source to which filmmakers turned for good plots. *The Day of the Jackal* (1973) imagines an assassination plot against French president Charles de Gaulle, following the shooter's methodical advance toward his target as the police scramble to catch him. Novelist Frederick Forsyth also drew upon historical authenticity for *The Odessa File*, adapted for film in 1974, as a journalist starts out trying to track down a real-life Nazi war criminal and uncovers evidence of a powerful group of former officers in Hitler's SS banded together to protect each other from discovery and prosecution. Nazi hunter Simon Wiesenthal served as a consultant on the film, and his tireless pursuit focused widespread attention on uncaptured Nazi war criminals, many of whom were said to live in South America—a major plot point in both *Marathon Man* (1976) and *The Boys from Brazil* (1978).

THE DAY OF THE JACKAL

Edward Fox was hired for the lead role in *The Day of the Jackal* (1973) after director Fred Zinnemann saw him in *The Go-Between* (1970). Although Fox was not widely known at the time, Zinnemann believed his relative obscurity would work in the film's favor, sustaining an air of mystery around the assassin.

WESTERNS

BUCK AND THE PREACHER

Harry Belafonte (left) and Sidney Poitier brace themselves for a shoot-out in *Buck and the Preacher* (1972). Although African-American filmmakers had been making westerns with all-black casts since the 1930s, Poitier's directing debut was the first such film to be released by a major Hollywood studio to nonsegregated theaters.

After more than four decades of acting in front of the camera, John Wayne finally got an Academy Award in the spring of 1970, for his performance as drunken, one-eyed U.S. Marshal Rooster Cogburn in *True Grit* (1969). "If I'd known this was all it would take," he exclaimed as he held the Oscar in his hands, "I'd have put that eyepatch on forty years ago."

Although Wayne was beginning to show signs of wear and tear, he still continued to make films during the first half of the 1970s, subtly adjusting his

THE COWBOYS

John Wayne assumes a familiar position in this 1972 western.

portrayal of the iconic western hero to accommodate his age and declining health. He became more of a father figure in films like *Big Jake* (1971) and *The Cowboys* (1972) but, at times, a flawed one; in *Cahill U.S. Marshal* (1973), his sons decide they have to rob a bank to get his attention. Wayne detoured briefly into the modern crime genre after watching a film he turned down, *Dirty Harry* (1971), become a huge hit for Clint Eastwood. His two cop films, *McQ* (1974) and *Brannigan* (1975) are clear imitations of Eastwood's no-nonsense vigilante—which of course owed much, in turn, to the protagonists of classic Wayne films like *The Searchers* (1956). After returning in *Rooster Cogburn* (1975) to the role that won him the Oscar, Wayne elected to end his career on a high note with *The Shootist* (1976).

THE BEGUILED

Clint Eastwood peers through the camera on the set of *The Beguiled*. The 1971 Civil War picture was actually directed by Don Siegel, but Eastwood was just about ready to helm his first picture, *Play Misty for Me* (1971), which was released later that year.

LITTLE BIG MAN

General Custer (Richard Mulligan) confronts Indian scout Jack Crabb (Dustin Hoffman) for leading him and the U.S. Cavalry into slaughter at the climax of *Little Big Man* (1970).

Richard Harris waits patiently while makeup artists work on the special effects that add that extra touch of realism to the scene in *A Man Called Horse* (1970) in which his character is suspended by hooks through his nipples (opposite). The ritual was based on extensive research into Sioux initiation rites.

Aging gunfighter John Bernard Books faces a situation much like Wayne's own, dying of cancer in a world that, although it readily acknowledges him as a legend, is rapidly passing him by and has little use for him. In that sense, *The Shootist*, like Sam Peckinpah's *The Wild Bunch* (1969), is an elegy for the western as well as for Wayne, and director Don Siegel packs the supporting cast with several instantly recognizable stars who had worked with Wayne before, including Hugh O'Brian, Richard Boone, John Carradine, and Jimmy Stewart.

"HISTORY IS NOTHING MORE THAN DISRESPECT FOR THE DEAD"

The western genre had allowed room for shades of moral ambiguity before the Vietnam War, but as millions of Americans came to question the rightness of the conflict, Hollywood began to poke more and more holes in the mythic history that had been handed down over the last century. Films such as *Little Big Man* (1970) and *Buffalo Bill and the Indians* (1976) openly mock legendary figures General Custer and Buffalo Bill Cody, *Doc* (1971) takes a less than reverent approach to the story of Wyatt Earp and Doc Holliday, and *Dirty Little Billy* (1972) and *Pat Garrett and Billy the Kid* (1973) make the outlaw even more of an antihero than he already was.

A MAN CALLED HORSE

Little Big Man was also one of the first films to take up the Native American perspective on how the West was won—or rather, a perspective sympathetic to the Native Americans, since Jack Crabb (Dustin Hoffman) is actually a white man who has been adopted into the Cheyenne tribe. The narrative strategy was a common one for filmmakers seeking to tell western stories from an outsider's viewpoint but forced by necessity to cast bankable stars in lead roles. Thus, Richard Harris played a British aristocrat who endures grueling tests of physical endurance to prove his worthiness to become a member of the Sioux Nation in *A Man Called Horse* (1970) and *The Return of a Man Called Horse* (1976). In *Jeremiah Johnson* (1972), Robert Redford stars, as a hermit trapper who briefly finds a home for himself in a forced marriage to a woman from the Flathead tribe.

African Americans also rose to a more prominent position within the genre during the early 1970s, and the black westerns often had pointed history lessons. *Buck and the Preacher*

BUFFALO BILL AND THE INDIANS

Kevin McCarthy (left) and Joel Grey flank Paul Newman in *Buffalo Bill and the Indians, or Sitting Bull's History Lesson* (1976). Robert Altman's second western came out just in time for America's bicentennial celebrations, but its revisionist take on the Wild West flopped at the box office.

(1972) and *Man and Boy* (1972), for example, deals frankly with the racism black settlers faced as they struggled to establish new homes in the West. Other movies were simply blaxploitation flicks with horses and six-shooters. Action star Fred Williamson made several such films, including *Take a Hard Ride* (1975), which reunited him with *Three the Hard Way* costars Jim Brown and Jim Kelly. Gordon Parks Jr., who had made his directing debut with *Superfly* (1972), applied that film's innovative montage techniques to an African-American variant on the Bonnie and Clyde story in *Thomasine and Bushrod* (1974), starring the real-life couple of Max Julien and Vonetta McGee.

HANNIE CAULDER

Raquel Welch bounced back from the 1970 flop *Myra Breckinridge* by starring in *Hannie Caulder*, in which she plays a woman who learns how to shoot a pistol so she can track down the bandits who raped her and murdered her husband.

THE ELECTRIC HORSEMAN

As washed-up rodeo star Sonny Steele, Robert Redford liberates a racehorse and rides down the streets of Las Vegas in *The Electric Horseman* (1979). The cynical comedy was Redford's fourth collaboration with director Sydney Pollack; the two had met in 1962, when they both made their movie-acting debuts in *War Hunt*.

A GUNFIGHT

Kirk Douglas and Johnny Cash chat on the set of *A Gunfight* (1971). Although this film is often cited as Cash's first acting role, he actually starred in the low-budget thriller *Five Minutes to Live* ten years earlier.

THE HIRED HAND

After the success of *Easy Rider* (1969), Peter Fonda was given the opportunity to direct *The Hired Hand* (1971). The western, in which he and Warren Oates play two drifters who make an effort at settling down, confounded Universal Pictures with its visual lyricism and minimalist narrative, and scenes were inserted to make the story line slightly more conventional.

BLAZING SADDLES

Gene Wilder and Cleavon Little confront each other as the Waco Kid and Black Bart in Mel Brooks's *Blazing Saddles* (1974). The streets of Rock Ridge may have looked familiar to filmgoers in 1974; Brooks shot on the same studio set Michael Crichton had used for *Westworld* (1973).

McCABE & MRS. MILLER

Warren Beatty and Julie Christie wait on the Vancouver set of *McCabe & Mrs. Miller* (1971) while the crew sets up a shot. Beatty reacted even more poorly to director Robert Altman's improvisational techniques than the stars of *M*A*S*H* had, but their collaboration transformed the western as profoundly as the other film had done war pictures.

JUNIOR BONNER

Steve McQueen is seen here in the title role of *Junior Bonner* (1972) with costars Ida Lupino, Joe Don Baker, and (facing away from the camera) Robert Preston; Sam Peckinpah's favorite among his own movies was one of several rodeo-themed films to come out in 1972. Others included *When the Legends Die*, starring Richard Widmark and Frederic Forrest, *J. W. Coop* (with Cliff Robertson), and *The Honkers* (James Coburn).

WHEN THE LEGENDS DIE

(1970), still managed to tweak the genre's conventions. And Jack Nicholson, who hadn't done a western since Monte Hellman's bleakly existential *The Shooting,* in 1967, turned in a pair of quirky performances in *The Missouri Breaks* (1976) and *Goin' South* (1978), directing the latter film himself.

"DYING AIN'T MUCH OF A LIVING"

If any one actor could be said to have inherited John Wayne's mantle as the first and foremost western star, however, it would have to be Clint Eastwood. His trilogy of "spaghetti westerns" (westerns produced in Italy) with Sergio Leone in the mid-1960s made him an international star, and he built on that image in subsequent films such as *Hang 'em High* (1968) and *Two Mules for Sister Sara* (1970)—even having a go at singing with Lee Marvin in *Paint Your Wagon* (1969). He did a few more westerns for other directors in the early 1970s, but with *High Plains Drifter* (1973), Eastwood began to take more direct control of his image, investing the ambiguity of the Man with No Name with a sense of eerie dread. *The Outlaw Josey Wales* (1976) presents an equally alienated antihero, a former Confederate soldier on the run after refusing to surrender to the Union troops that murdered his family.

Character actor Michael J. Pollard (left) played a rare lead role in *Dirty Little Billy* (1972), starring as a juvenile delinquent version of Billy Bonney. Falling in with the wrong element in the form of petty criminal Goldie (Richard Evans, right), Bonney takes the first steps toward his eventual notoriety as Billy the Kid.

DIRTY LITTLE BILLY

THE MISSOURI BREAKS

Jack Nicholson and Marlon Brando costarred in *The Missouri Breaks* (1976). After the back-to-back success of *The Godfather* and *Last Tango in Paris* (both 1972), Brando dropped out of acting for a few years, returning here in a quirky performance as a bounty hunter who occasionally wears women's clothing and has an unusually close relationship with his horse.

ULTRA-COOL ACTOR
JAMES COBURN

"I believe only in dynamite."

James Coburn got his start in Hollywood acting in westerns, playing opposite Randolph Scott in *Ride Lonesome* and Fred MacMurray in *Face of a Fugitive* (both 1959). His big break came in 1960, when he costarred in *The Magnificent Seven,* and although he would branch out into a number of genres during the following decade (most notably the spy film, where he out-Bonded Bond as *Our Man Flint*), he would frequently return to the saddle.

Duck, You Sucker (1971)—also known as *Once Upon a Time in the Revolution* and *A Fistful of Dynamite*—was the last western on which Sergio Leone took a director's credit. The tale of a collaboration between Coburn's IRA explosives man and Rod Steiger's Mexican revolutionary was originally slated to be directed by Peter Bogdanovich, but he left the production after it became clear that Leone was too hands-on a producer for his tastes. Coburn returned to Europe to make *A Reason to Live, A Reason to Die* (1972) and then signed on with Sam Peckinpah to costar in *Pat Garrett and Billy the Kid* (1973) as the newly appointed sheriff forced to hunt down his former friend. After that, he took part in a long-distance horse race with Gene Hackman in *Bite the Bullet* (1975) and played an escaped convict out for vengeance against the lawman who sent him to prison in *The Last Hard Men* (1976).

DUCK, YOU SUCKER

THE MISSOURI BREAKS

Jack Nicholson and Marlon Brando costarred in *The Missouri Breaks* (1976). After the back-to-back success of *The Godfather* and *Last Tango in Paris* (both 1972), Brando dropped out of acting for a few years, returning here in a quirky performance as a bounty hunter who occasionally wears women's clothing and has an unusually close relationship with his horse.

ULTRA-COOL ACTOR
JAMES COBURN

"I believe only in dynamite."

James Coburn got his start in Hollywood acting in westerns, playing opposite Randolph Scott in *Ride Lonesome* and Fred MacMurray in *Face of a Fugitive* (both 1959). His big break came in 1960, when he costarred in *The Magnificent Seven*, and although he would branch out into a number of genres during the following decade (most notably the spy film, where he out-Bonded Bond as *Our Man Flint*), he would frequently return to the saddle.

Duck, You Sucker (1971)—also known as *Once Upon a Time in the Revolution* and *A Fistful of Dynamite*—was the last western on which Sergio Leone took a director's credit. The tale of a collaboration between Coburn's IRA explosives man and Rod Steiger's Mexican revolutionary was originally slated to be directed by Peter Bogdanovich, but he left the production after it became clear that Leone was too hands-on a producer for his tastes. Coburn returned to Europe to make *A Reason to Live, A Reason to Die* (1972) and then signed on with Sam Peckinpah to costar in *Pat Garrett and Billy the Kid* (1973) as the newly appointed sheriff forced to hunt down his former friend. After that, he took part in a long-distance horse race with Gene Hackman in *Bite the Bullet* (1975) and played an escaped convict out for vengeance against the lawman who sent him to prison in *The Last Hard Men* (1976).

DUCK, YOU SUCKER

The most famous appearance by a black actor in a 1970s western, however, would have to be Cleavon Little's portrayal of Black Bart, the farcical hero of *Blazing Saddles* (1974). Director Mel Brooks and his team of screenwriters (including stand-up comic Richard Pryor) confronted the racism issue head-on, from the casual disregard for the black railroad crew to the startled reaction of the people of Rock Ridge when their new sheriff rides into town. Although there was a long tradition of poking fun at westerns, from Bob Hope in *The Paleface* (1948) to its remake with Don Knotts in *The Shakiest Gun in the West* (1968), *Blazing Saddles* took advantage of looser restrictions on film content, piling on sexual innuendos and other forms of raunchy humor, most notably the cowpokes farting around an open campfire. Harvey Korman's devious robber baron Hedley Lamarr and Madeline Kahn's Academy Award–nominated characterization of Lili von Shtupp, the lusty showgirl with a heart of gold, further pushed stereotypical western characters to comedic extremes.

Comedians weren't the only ones taking part in such send-ups. After Lee Marvin got an Oscar for his lead role in *Cat Ballou* (1965), more actors took an interest in westerns with an amusing edge. John Wayne had shown a humorous side before *True Grit*, but he proved willing to gently mock his heroic image at unprecedented length by playing Rooster Cogburn. Gene Kelly's one foray into the genre was directing *The Cheyenne Social Club* (1970), in which Henry Fonda and James Stewart played old cowpokes stymied when one of them inherits his brother's bordello. James Garner went from playing Wyatt Earp in *Hour of the Gun* (1967) to starring in *Support Your Local Sheriff!* (1969) as a wanderer who takes the badge strictly for the pay; the comedy proved so successful that director Burt Kennedy was able to reunite the cast to poke fun at *A Fistful of Dollars* (1964) in *Support Your Local Gunfighter* (1972); Kennedy also used many of the same supporting actors in the Frank Sinatra vehicle *Dirty Dingus Magee* (1970). The Wild West of the seventies was filled with comic flimflam artists, from James Garner and Louis Gossett in *Skin*

JEREMIAH JOHNSON

Jeremiah Johnson was shot on location throughout the state of Utah, including the Sundance ski resort, which would become the home of Robert Redford's innovative festival for independent filmmakers.

RED SUN

Toshiro Mifune sneaks up on Alain Delon, adding a new twist to the western showdown in *Red Sun*. The film had been a hit in Europe for nearly a year before it was finally released in the United States in 1972; it would remain a cult favorite in France throughout the decade.

PAT GARRETT AND BILLY THE KID

James Coburn as lawman Pat Garrett looms over the corpse of his former friend, Billy the Kid (Kris Kristofferson), in Sam Peckinpah's elegiac 1973 film, which contained elements of the distinctive approach to cinematic violence he displayed in his 1969 hit, *The Wild Bunch*.

THE BALLAD OF CABLE HOGUE

Director Sam Peckinpah (top center) and Jason Robards (on horse) wait to shoot a scene from *The Ballad of Cable Hogue* (1970). The tale of Hogue, a prospector left to die in the desert by unscrupulous colleagues who miraculously finds water, buys the land around the well, and waits for the moment he can get revenge on his ex-partners, suprised audiences expecting another bloodbath from Peckinpah.

Game (1971) to George Segal and Goldie Hawn in *The Duchess and the Dirtwater Fox* (1976). And Gene Wilder, who had so effectively mocked the alcoholic gunslinger stereotype in *Blazing Saddles*, added a new twist to the genre as *The Frisco Kid* (1979), an Orthodox rabbi braving highwaymen and Indians on the path to his congregation in San Francisco.

Robert Altman's *McCabe & Mrs. Miller* (1971) and John Huston's *The Life and Times of Judge Roy Bean* (1972) take a subtler approach but, like Sam Peckinpah's *The Ballad of Cable Hogue*

But that would be Eastwood's last western for nearly a decade, mirroring a trend throughout Hollywood. Where westerns had once been a regular feature at movie theaters, they now became an increasingly rare event; by the late 1980s, it would be considered noteworthy for an actor of any stature to do a big-screen western at all. Although some of the blame can be laid upon *Heaven's Gate* (1980), even a box-office disaster that notorious couldn't have scared away every producer in the industry. In fact, the genre continued to flourish in made-for-television movies, proving that money wasn't the problem. Perhaps the revisionists had done their job too well, undercutting the familiar myths until the genre itself became almost unbelievable—and little comfort for audiences looking for an escape from the upheavals of their contemporary world.

THE OUTLAW JOSEY WALES

Clint Eastwood took over the direction of *The Outlaw Josey Wales* (1976) when he grew displeased with Philip Kaufman's take on the material. After the resulting controversy, the Directors Guild of America declared that no filmmaker could be replaced midshoot by anyone else working on the production, a policy that became known as the "Eastwood rule."

HEISTS, CONS

THE HOT ROCK

Robert Redford and George Segal (front and back) bust into prison to get Paul Sand (center) *out* in one of several break-ins master thief John Dortmunder must execute to get his hands on a priceless diamond in *The Hot Rock* (1972).

& CAPERS

THE STING

Paul Newman and Robert Redford are the old pro and the rookie who team up for the most famous of Hollywood's big cons in *The Sting* (1973). The film won seven Academy Awards, including best director and best picture; Edith Head also won the last of her eight Oscars for designing these outfits and other costumes evocative of 1930s Chicago.

Screenwriter David S. Ward was doing research on pickpockets for his first film, *Steelyard Blues* (1972), when he stumbled onto some material about grifters who specialized in the big con—an elaborate setup designed to fleece one victim out of a large sum of money all at once. Recognizing a good story when he saw one, he began working on a new script, called *The Sting*, about a young con artist who teams up with a seasoned veteran to exact revenge against the gangster who killed his mentor. The part was written with Robert Redford in mind, and although the actor hesitated at first, he eventually signed on. Director George Roy Hill got hold of the script and asked to direct, and from there it took only a conversation with Paul Newman to reunite the stars and director of *Butch Cassidy and the Sundance Kid*.

THE FRIENDS OF EDDIE COYLE

Robert Mitchum and Peter Boyle enjoy a hockey game at Boston Garden in *The Friends of Eddie Coyle* (1973).

As one of the first great comic-action duos, Redford and Newman had helped turn *Butch* into the biggest hit of 1969. *The Sting* (1973) outgrossed it by nearly half, $78.1 million to $45.9 million, beating out every other film that year except for *The Exorcist*. The film's good fortune was contagious: Marvin Hamlisch's theme "The Entertainer," based on a tune by ragtime composer Scott Joplin, reached number three on the Billboard charts, while Robert Shaw, as the gangster

Doyle Lonnegan, found the first in a string of commercially successful roles. Ten years later, Ward would revisit the characters for *The Sting II*, but without Hill or any of the lead actors, the sequel was dead on arrival at theaters.

"WHAT DO YOU THINK THIS IS, A WESTERN?"

The first and most obvious trend inspired by *Butch Cassidy and the Sundance Kid* was the rise of the buddy film, combining the best elements of comedy duos and action movies. Prominent team-ups include Clint Eastwood and Jeff Bridges in *Thunderbolt and Lightfoot* (1974) and Gene Wilder and Richard Pryor in *Silver Streak* (1976), but a broad definition of the genre might include pairings such as Alan Arkin and Peter Falk (*The In-Laws*, 1979) and even Donny and Marie Osmond (*Goin' Coconuts*, 1978).

Another side effect of the popularity of *Butch* was a string of robberies set in the Old West and other historic locales. Men had robbed banks and trains on screen before Butch and Sundance, of course, but rarely as the ostensible heroes of the picture. Gritty "spaghetti westerns" such as *A Man Called Sledge* and *Sabata* were matched by American productions such as *El Condor* and *Two Mules for Sister Sara* (all 1970). *Harry and Walter Go to New York* (1976) tried to combine elements of both Redford/Newman hits, with James Caan and Elliott Gould as failed con men who try their hand at a bank job. Later, *The Great Train Robbery* (1979) would prove that Victorian England's thieves were as full of bravado as any western outlaw.

The Great Depression also proved fertile ground for cinematic imagination. A number of films tried more or less to emulate the standard set by the groundbreaking *Bonnie and Clyde* (1967), with Robert Altman perhaps coming closest in *Thieves Like Us* (1973). Roger Corman's American International Pictures got great mileage out of the real-life exploits of Ma Barker (*Bloody Mama*, 1970), Bertha Thompson (*Boxcar Bertha*, 1972), and John Dillinger (*Dillinger*, 1973). Corman's next production company, New World Pictures, went back to the Dillinger saga for *The Lady in Red* (1979). Meanwhile, Larry Cohen was busy mining *The Private Files of J. Edgar Hoover* (1977).

PAPILLON

Steve McQueen (left) plays the title role in *Papillon* (1973), based on the memoirs of self-professed Devil's Island inmate Henri Charrière. As his sidekick, Dustin Hoffman had to wear glasses so thick he required corrective contact lenses so he could see clearly.

CHARLEY VERRICK

Andrew Robinson (left) and Walter Matthau count out the money from their bank job in *Charley Verrick* (1973). Because the bank they rob turns out to be a front for organized crime, they're hunted down by a hit man, played by Joe Don Baker.

THE BRINK'S JOB

Peter Falk (center) starred in *The Brink's Job* (1978), based on a real-life robbery in which a group of small-time Boston hoods managed to outwit Brink's vaunted security system and get away with nearly $3 million. Some of the actual thieves served as technical advisers on the film.

DOG DAY AFTERNOON

Al Pacino looks on while *Dog Day Afternoon* (1975) director Sidney Lumet surveys the scene outside the Brooklyn bank used for location shooting. Lumet and Pacino were both nominated for Academy Awards, as was the picture, but *One Flew Over the Cuckoo's Nest* won in all three categories that year; *Dog Day* received its only Oscar for Frank Pierson's screenplay.

"I'M ROBBING A BANK BECAUSE THEY GOT MONEY HERE"

THEY GOT MONEY HERE

Following the lead of European filmmakers unencumbered by Hays Code restrictions on "acceptable" content, in the 1960s Hollywood kicked off a genre of heist films that went into previously forbidden detail explaining how the crimes were committed. By the end of the decade, those details had become so fetishized that the elaborate schemes concocted in films such as *$* and *The Anderson Tapes* (both 1971) were treated as cinematic set pieces, as much of a reason to see the films as the actors perpetrating the crimes.

In other films, however, the criminal was still the main focus. Although Peckinpah paid his usual meticulous attention to the action scenes, his adaptation of Jim Thompson's *The Getaway* (1972) places equal emphasis on the relationship between paroled thief Doc McCoy and his wife, Carol (played by Steve McQueen and Ali McGraw, who became real-life lovers during the shoot and later married). In *Straight Time* (1978), Dustin Hoffman played a career criminal modeled closely after Eddie Bunker, who wrote the novel on which the film is based after doing his own stretch for armed robbery. Sidney Lumet's *Dog Day Afternoon* (1975) focuses on the media circus surrounding a failed bank job that turns into a prolonged standoff, drawing upon the real-life drama of a Brooklyn thief who attempted to steal money to pay for a

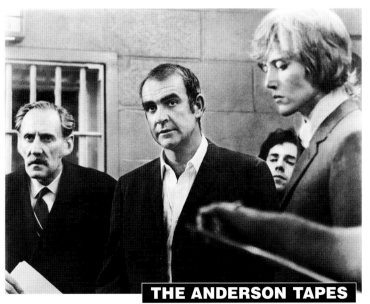

THE ANDERSON TAPES

Christopher Walken (right) was introduced to film audiences in *The Anderson Tapes* (1971), playing a sidekick to Sean Connery. He was, however, an old hand at showbiz by then, having begun his career as a child actor on TV in the 1950s and costarring with Liza Minnelli in the off-Broadway musical *Best Foot Forward* when he was twenty years old.

THE GREAT TRAIN ROBBERY

Sean Connery and Donald Sutherland starred as the mastermind and chief accomplice behind the first successful heist of a moving train in *The Great Train Robbery* (1979), adapted by writer-director Michael Crichton from his own novel.

THEY MIGHT BE GIANTS

Although many films were made about Sherlock Holmes in the 1970s, one of the most memorable is about the man who thought he *was* Holmes: George C. Scott with Joanne Woodward in *They Might Be Giants* (1971).

MURDER ON THE ORIENT EXPRESS

Although Agatha Christie's stories had been filmed many times before (Albert Finney was, in fact, the third actor to play master detective Hercule Poirot on-screen), *Murder on the Orient Express* (1974) set a new standard for populating her mysteries with an all-star cast; she liked it best of all the films made from her books.

SLEUTH

The 1972 film version of Anthony Shaffer's play *Sleuth* became the first movie in which the entire cast, Laurence Olivier and Michael Caine (in clown mask), was nominated for Academy Awards; both men were up for best actor, which went to Marlon Brando for *The Godfather*.

lover's sex change operation (although his name was changed to Sonny Wortzik in the film).

Most motivations for turning to a life of crime were not quite so outlandish as Sonny's. With the economy in turmoil, several films got laughs out of the idea that ordinary citizens could relieve their financial burdens with a little larceny. *Fun with Dick and Jane* (1977) presents a married couple who turn to robbery when unemployment checks fail to cover their household expenses, while a trio of housewives band together in *How to Beat the High Cost of Living* (1980). The three elderly men living on Social Security in *Going in Style* (1979) can certainly use the money they get from robbing a bank, but that's not nearly as important to them as breaking up the monotony of their lives.

GOING IN STYLE

Lee Strasberg, George Burns, and Art Carney (left to right) are the senior citizens turned bank robbers in *Going in Style* (1979). The three men would share the Venice Film Festival's award for best actor that year.

ULTRA-COOL ACTOR
PAM GRIER

"This game is called survival. Let's see how well you can play it."

Pam Grier was a premed college student in Denver when she entered a beauty pageant to try to make some extra money. A third-place finish led to other contests and the eventual attention of a Hollywood agent. Her first major role was in *The Big Doll House* (1971), a women-in-prison film that launched her long (and rewarding) relationships with producer Roger Corman and director Jack Hill. The low-budget flick was shot on location in the Philippines, as were several of Grier's following pictures, the perfectly titled *Women in Cages* (1971), *Black Mama, White Mama* (1972), and *The Big Bird Cage* (1972). At some point during these productions, she survived a near-fatal bout with a tropical disease, enduring temporary blindness and hair loss before fully recovering.

Back at full strength, Grier solidified her position as the female action star of the seventies, with a pair of films directed by Hill: *Coffy* (1973) and *Foxy Brown* (1974). By 1975, at the height of her fame, she became the first African-American woman to appear on the cover of *Ms.* magazine, but the "Queen of Blaxploitation" was about to find her kingdom dwindling. Her film work for the decade ended with a weighty role in the Richard Pryor vehicle *Greased Lightning* (1977), after which she joined the all-star cast of the 1979 miniseries *Roots: The Next Generations*. After that, she began building a new career as a solid character actress, until a wave of blaxploitation nostalgia in the mid nineties brought her back into the spotlight, resulting in a Golden Globe nomination for her lead performance in Quentin Tarantino's *Jackie Brown* (1997).

FOXY BROWN

CLEOPATRA JONES

Although Pam Grier was the female action star of the 1970s, former model Tamara Dobson came close to offering her some competition in *Cleopatra Jones* (1973), but Dobson's acting career never really took off after the film's sequel.

BOXCAR BERTHA

Roger Corman gave fledgling director Martin Scorsese roughly $600,000 to make one of American International Pictures' typical exploitation flicks. The result was *Boxcar Bertha* (1972), starring Barbara Hershey and David Carradine as union activists who turn to a life of crime to strike back at the railroad corporations. The grisly fate that befalls Carradine's character would hint at themes that recur throughout the director's films.

CAGED HEAT

Jonathan Demme made his directing debut with *Caged Heat* (1974), one of many seventies films about women in prison (usually dressed rather skimpily) that treated the abandonment of the Hays Code as an opportunity to load films with bare breasts, very thinly veiled lesbianism, and rape scenes. Although Demme would eventually move on to more prestigious projects like *The Silence of the Lambs* and *Philadelphia*, he remained true to his roots by continuing to work with Tak Fujimoto, the cinematographer on this first project.

As overall cinematic violence intensified during the 1970s, movie prisons became much more brutal places. George Kennedy, who had won an Oscar for playing a sadistic corrections officer in *Cool Hand Luke* (1967), went back on the job for *Mean Dog Blues* (1973), this time using inmates as fodder for his fighting dogs. *Short Eyes* (1977) was filmed on location at Riker's Island; screenwriter Miguel Pinero had written the story about the victimization of an accused child molester by other inmates in a Sing Sing writer's workshop while doing time on a robbery conviction. *Terminal Island* (1973) dispenses with all the niceties, dumping California's inmates on an island to fend for themselves; John Carpenter would use a similar plot device nearly a decade later in *Escape from New York* (1981).

UPTOWN SATURDAY NIGHT

Sidney Poitier and Bill Cosby made three hit comedies, all of which were also directed by Poitier. Their first pairing, *Uptown Saturday Night* (1974), had them scrambling to recover a winning lottery ticket after it gets stolen in a nightclub heist. In *Let's Do It Again* (1975), the two became con artists who have to rig a boxing match twice—first to take the winnings and then to hand them back to the gangsters they fleeced. Finally, in *A Piece of the Action* (1977), the duo are blackmailed into going straight and then blackmailed again into doing one last job.

THIEVES LIKE US

Robert Altman relaxes on the set of *Thieves Like Us* (1974) with costars Shelley Duvall (left) and Louise Fletcher. Although Duvall was already a regular member of Altman's repertory-style core cast, this was Fletcher's first experience with the director, who was so impressed by Fletcher's relationship with her deaf parents that he began to create a part in his next film, *Nashville* (1975), with her in mind. When contract negotiations between the two broke down, that role went to Lily Tomlin, in her first motion-picture role.

THE OUTFIT

Robert Duvall (left) stars as a thief who turns to an old friend (Joe Don Baker, right) for help in fighting off the mob. The Richard Stark novel upon which the 1973 movie was based was actually a sequel to *Point Blank*, necessitating a name change for Duvall's character in order to distinguish it from Lee Marvin's 1967 film.

DEATH WISH

Charles Bronson stands before a thematically apt billboard while shooting *Death Wish* (1974). Although Bronson would become identified with the role of architect-turned-vigilante Paul Kersey, it was actually eight years before he agreed to make the first of the film's four sequels.

MIDNIGHT EXPRESS

Brad Davis plays Billy Hayes in *Midnight Express* (1978), based on Hayes's book about his experiences in the Turkish prison system after being arrested on drug charges. Oliver Stone won the first of three Academy Awards for his screenplay, although the film's depiction of the Turks remains controversial to this day.

ULTRA-COOL ACTOR
SHELLEY WINTERS

"In the water, I'm a very skinny lady."

Five years after winning the Academy Award for her supporting role in *A Patch of Blue*, Shelley Winters kicked off the 1970s with Roger Corman's *Bloody Mama*. It wasn't her first acting job with American International Pictures, the masters of the exploitation film, nor would it be her last. In 1968, she had played the mother of the evil young president in the political satire *Wild in the Streets;* in 1971, she is the witch in a modern version of Hansel and Gretel called *Whoever Slew Auntie Roo?* In *Bloody Mama,* she starred as Ma Barker, with a quartet of young, largely unknown actors (including a young Robert De Niro) playing the sons who made up her gang. Winters did a good enough job as a criminal mastermind that she was tapped to play Mommy, the sadistic drug dealer who tries to take down a government agent in *Cleopatra Jones* (1973).

Winters would continue to work on prestigious productions throughout the decade, getting good supporting parts from directors such as Paul Mazursky (*Blume in Love,* 1973) and Roman Polanski (*The Tenant,* 1976). *The Poseidon Adventure* (1972) earned her another Oscar nomination, but her later forays into the disaster genre were simply disasters, for example, the *Jaws* knockoff *Tentacles* (1977). Apart from her star turn in *Poseidon,* perhaps the most recognizable of her performances from the seventies, at least for younger viewers, is as the evil matron in the Disney musical *Pete's Dragon* (1977).

CLEOPATRA JONES

THE KING OF MARVIN GARDENS

By all rights, *The King of Marvin Gardens* (1972) should have been a success, with Ellen Burstyn (left) and Bruce Dern joining the reunion of Jack Nicholson and director Bob Rafelson, who had made *Five Easy Pieces* (1970) together. Despite critical acclaim, however, the downbeat drama didn't quite connect with audiences unused to seeing Nicholson as the quiet brother.

As one might expect, most characters in prison want to get out as quickly as possible. Almost every women's-prison flick, for example, has been an escape story; the most notable, *Black Mama, White Mama* (1971), had Pam Grier and Margaret Markov shackled together like a distaff version of the characters in *The Defiant Ones* (1958). In *Riot* (1969), Gene Hackman ropes Jim Brown into a scheme to cover up an escape attempt with a phony riot among the inmates; Brown would have to break out again in *The Slams* (1973), this time to recover his stolen loot before the hiding place is demolished. *Papillon* (1973) teamed Steve McQueen and Dustin Hoffman as French convicts who make repeated efforts to escape from Devil's Island, although Roger Corman managed to rush *I Escaped from Devil's Island* into theaters two months earlier. And Clint Eastwood reenacted one of America's most notorious breakouts in *Escape from Alcatraz* (1979)—with an open ending that suggests Frank Morris's actual escape attempt in 1962 might not have failed after all.

HARD CRIME

TAXI DRIVER

Robert De Niro may have spent a month working twelve-hour shifts driving a New York City cab to prepare himself for the role of Travis Bickle in *Taxi Driver* (1976), but he wasn't about to shave his head. Makeup artists created the iconic Mohawk by gluing a bald cap to De Niro's head and adding horsehair.

Paramount's original plans for *The Godfather* (1972) included updating the plot of Mario Puzo's novel and setting it in a contemporary midwestern city such as Kansas City or St. Louis. With that in mind, the studio budgeted only $2.5 million for the entire production and hired a young director, Francis Ford Coppola, with a track record on small movies. Coppola had his own ideas about the film, however, beginning with an insistence on filming Puzo's story of the Corleone family's solidification of their hold on New York's criminal underworld in its original post–World War II setting—and although this decision became more acceptable as the book became a best-

MEAN STREETS

Harvey Keitel kneels in the middle of a Brooklyn street at the end of *Mean Streets* (1973).

seller, the studio was less than thrilled about the added costs in making a period picture, which along with other expenses swelled the final budget to approximately $6 million.

Whatever Coppola wanted, the producers' first reaction was to reject it. They didn't want Al Pacino to play Michael Corleone; they didn't even want Marlon Brando as the family patriarch. Coppola was forced to film a "makeup test" of Brando that was, in reality, a screen test to convince Paramount he could do the part. Even after production had started, the studio made its dissatisfaction felt so strongly that Coppola believed he would be fired at any moment. When *The French Connection* was released

THE GODFATHER

The Godfather (1972) crew technicians put nearly 150 squibs on James Caan's body to simulate the bullets ripping him apart during this tollbooth execution. The scene was shot with several cameras in one take at the Robert Moses Causeway, which was actually still in the planning stages in 1947, the "official" date of Sonny Corleone's death.

THE FRENCH CONNECTION

Gene Hackman stars as Jimmy "Popeye" Doyle in *The French Connection* (1971), with Roy Scheider (holding the shotgun) as his partner, Buddy Russo. The two actors spent a month with Eddie Egan, the New York cop on whom the character of Popeye is based, to research their parts, and they would later abandon their scripted dialogue to use the terminology they had learned from the police officers they met.

while he was working on the final edit of his film, Coppola was despondent, convinced his sprawling film, which ran just shy of three hours, wasn't anywhere near as good.

The huge popularity of *The Godfather* in theaters and at the Academy Awards—the film won best picture and best adapted screenplay, Brando famously sent a Native American actress to refuse his Oscar, and three of the five nominations for best supporting actor were taken by Pacino and costars James Caan and Robert Duvall—proved Coppola wrong. The painful experience of working with Paramount, however, made him reluctant to direct a sequel, and it was only when the studio rejected his offer to produce the film if Martin Scorsese could direct that he came back. His newly acquired clout as a hitmaker gave him a budget nearly double that for the first movie, which he used to make a film that ran nearly a half hour longer. *The Godfather, Part II* (1974) would earn Coppola Oscars for producing, directing, and cowriting the film with Puzo. Robert De Niro, who had unsuccessfully tested for the part of Sonny Corleone in the first film, won the best supporting award as a young Vito in flashbacks that paralleled the inner disintegration of Michael and the Corleone family. That emotional melodrama—the gradual revelation of Michael Corleone as a grand tragic figure—was a key element in the success of the *Godfather* saga that most "mob pictures" made in its wake couldn't quite emulate, emphasizing as they often did the distinctive on-screen violence.

Dino de Laurentiis was one of the first producers to take *The Godfather* head-on, rushing *The Valachi Papers* (1972), with Charles Bronson as real-life mob informant Joe Valachi, into theaters only eight months after Coppola's film. History also provided stories for *Lucky Luciano*, an Italian production dubbed into English and released to U.S. theaters in 1974, and *Capone* (1975), starring Ben Gazzara as the Chicago gangster.

The year between the two *Godfather* installments, 1973, was a good one for mob pictures. *The Stone Killer* featured Bronson as a detective out to stop a mafia plot clearly intended to evoke Michael Corleone's elimination of the heads of the "five families." Anthony Quinn headlined in *The Don Is Dead* as a mob boss out to avenge the murder of his mistress, while *The Seven-Ups* focused on a squad of undercover cops who need to figure out who is

SHAFT

Before Richard Roundtree landed the lead role in *Shaft* (1971), Gordon Parks had auditioned Ron O'Neal and Isaac Hayes. Hayes's tryout was so impressive that he was invited to compose the film's score and ended up winning an Academy Award for the theme song. O'Neal was rejected because he was considered too light skinned for the part, but Gordon Parks Jr. would go on to cast the actor in his film *Superfly* (1972).

SUPERFLY

COTTON COMES TO HARLEM

Cotton Comes to Harlem (1970) was one of the first significant African-American films with an urban focus, but the casting reflected writer-director Ossie Davis's background in theater. Calvin Lockhart (left) acted with the Royal Shakespeare Company during the 1960s, while Redd Foxx had been doing stand-up comedy for nearly thirty years.

THE WANDERERS

THE WARRIORS

Ken Wahl (second from left) starred as Richie, the leader of *The Wanderers* (1979). Philip Kaufman's film was based on a Richard Price novel about Bronx gang life in the 1960s. *The Warriors,* released the same year, got its story from a novel by Sol Yurick, who dealt with New York street gangs as a city welfare worker in the 1950s. Although it appears to be a superficial action yarn, the story is in fact a modern retelling of the defeated Greek army's retreat from Babylon in 401 B.C.

kidnapping New York kingpins and blaming them for it—while offering Roy Scheider his first lead role after notable supporting performances as Jane Fonda's pimp in *Klute* and Gene Hackman's partner on the police force in *The French Connection* (both 1971).

"YOU'VE GOT TO ASK YOURSELF ONE QUESTION: DO I FEEL LUCKY?"

Tough cops flourished at the movies in 1971: while Gene Hackman won the Oscar patrolling the streets of New York City as Popeye Doyle, Clint Eastwood filmed *Dirty Harry* in San Francisco—which is also where Sidney Poitier reprised the role of Virgil Tibbs, first seen in *In the Heat of the Night* (1967), for *The Organization* (1971). (Never mind that the first film had established the character as a Philadelphia cop; when the sequel *They Call Me MISTER Tibbs!* came out in 1970, he had been relocated without explanation.) This was also the year veteran Los Angeles police officer Joseph Wambaugh published his first novel, *The New Centurions*, subsequently made into a movie starring George C. Scott and Stacy Keach. His next novel, *The Blue Knight*, was filmed for television with William Holden in 1973, then again with George Kennedy two years later as the pilot for a short-lived series. By then, Wambaugh had retired from the force to concentrate on writing full time, but his books continued to present stories rooted in the experiences he shared with former colleagues. Hollywood's enthusiasm for his work remained strong, as seen in *The Choirboys* (1977) and *The Onion Field* (1979).

Hardnosed police officers, especially those willing to bend the rules to get criminals off the streets, were consistently popular with audiences, many of whom had to deal with rising crime rates in their own communities. The real-life story of Buford Pusser, a Tennessee sheriff whose no-nonsense approach to cleaning up his county led to at least one attempt on his life, inspired the movie *Walking Tall* (1973) and its two sequels. For those citizens who wished they could take the law into their own hands, *Death Wish* (1974) was the perfect fantasy, as Charles Bronson wages a one-man war on crime, frustrating the police with his ruthless efficiency against the criminal element. The movie *Joe* (1970), however, revealed the dark side of such fantasies while exposing their roots in conservative resentment of the counterculture's increasing influence.

GET CARTER

An Oscar nominee for his star turn in *Alfie* (1966), Michael Caine was well known to American audiences when he made *Get Carter* in 1971, even though almost all of his work had been in British films. It would take a few more years—and another Academy Award nomination—before he fully clicked with American studios.

SERPICO

Between the first two *Godfather* films, Al Pacino starred as undercover New York City cop Frank Serpico in Sidney Lumet's 1973 film. Much of the movie was shot in reverse sequence; Pacino grew his hair and beard out to shoot later scenes first, after which the production worked backward through the script, trimming him as they went.

BORN TO WIN

Czech-born filmmaker Ivan Passer wrote the screenplays for many of Milos Forman's 1960s films. The two
came to the United States at roughly the same time,
and Passer made his American debut as the writer
and director of *Born to Win* (1971), with George Segal
and Jay Fletcher as heroin addicts whose every action
is motivated by their twin desires to stay alive and
score their next fix. His next film, *Law and Disorder*
(1974), costarred Ernest Borgnine and Carroll
O'Connor as New York crime victims who join the aux-
iliary police force.

LAW AND DISORDER

Blaxploitation films mined film audiences' twin enthusiasm for hard crime and tough justice ruthlessly. Films such as *Superfly* (1972) and *Black Caesar* (1973) glamorized their drug-dealing protagonists, even as *Shaft* (1971) and *Gordon's War* (1973) set their heroes on crusades against organized crime. Some of these films were remakes recast with black actors; *Hit Man* (1972), for example, was *Get Carter* (1971) with Bernie Casey in the Michael Caine part. They would, in turn, influence filmmakers throughout the 1970s; the criminal underworlds in movies written or directed by Paul Schrader, from *The Yakuza* (1975) to *Hardcore* (1979), might not be quite as gritty without the precedents established at the beginning of the decade.

"YOU DON'T MAKE UP FOR YOUR SINS IN CHURCH"

Martin Scorsese shot his first feature-length film, *Who's That Knocking at My Door?* in and around the Lower East Side neighborhood where he grew up—and not all that far from New York University's film school, where he had started out making short subjects that melded the twin influences of NYU's documentarian approach and the art-film subculture of the late 1950s and early 1960s. After the film was released, in 1967, Scorsese went to Hollywood and took the occasional editing job while struggling to make another film. He was hired to direct *The Honeymoon Killers* (1970) and then taken off the project shortly after shooting began, but he eventually landed a directing gig with Roger Corman, who gave him four weeks to shoot *Boxcar Bertha* (1972). It was an invaluable experience in professional filmmaking, but the final

ACROSS 110TH STREET

Anthony Quinn (left) starred in *Across 110th Street* (1972), directed by Barry Shear. Shear started out in television in the 1950s and was only briefly a director for the big screen, making four movies between 1968 and 1973. After he returned to television, he directed many of the decade's top crime dramas, from *Police Story* to *Starsky and Hutch*.

"I know it was you, Fredo."

The first milestone of South Bronx native Al Pacino's acting career was his acceptance into the Actors Studio in 1966, where he studied under legendary teacher Lee Strasberg (who would later play opposite his pupil in *The Godfather, Part II*). A string of performances off and on Broadway led to a small part in the 1969 film *Me, Natalie*, after which he starred as a junkie who drags his girlfriend down to his level of addiction in *The Panic in Needle Park* (1971). When the producers of *The Godfather* initially balked at casting Pacino in the role of Michael Corleone, Coppola showed them *Panic* to convince them he was good enough to carry the dramatic weight of the part.

Between the two *Godfather* films, he went back to work for *Panic* director Jerry Schatzberg in *Scarecrow* (1973), as a discharged sailor who hooks up with an ex-con (Gene Hackman) and gets caught in a downward spiral. That same year, he starred in Sidney Lumet's *Serpico;* his performance as the undercover cop who blew the whistle on his corrupt colleagues in the New York police department resulted in his second Oscar nomination in as many years. He would also be nominated the following two years, for *The Godfather, Part II* and *Dog Day Afternoon*, and again at the end of the decade for . . . *And Justice for All* (1979), although the actual prize would elude him until the midnineties. The one movie during the 1970s that didn't cast him in connection to the criminal underworld or the justice system was *Bobby Deerfield* (1977), in which he played a race-car driver who falls in love with a dying woman—it was his only flop of the decade. (He did, however, finally learn how to drive in order to play the part.)

THE PANIC IN NEEDLE PARK

product was not exactly the type of film Scorsese wanted to spend his career making. Friends like John Cassavetes recognized this and urged him to develop more personal projects.

Scorsese returned to a script he had been working on for several years based loosely on his life as an adolescent and young adult in New York's Little Italy, where the presence of organized crime was simply accepted as a given, a state of affairs with which each person had to reconcile himself as he saw fit. Corman was interested in the script but asked Scorsese to make the characters black and move the action to Harlem to capitalize on the newly emerging blaxploitation market. Scorsese balked and, scraping the money together by alternate means, shot much of the movie in his old neighborhood, rehiring Harvey Keitel, the star of his first film, and signing Robert De Niro for the other male lead. His father pulled a few strings to deal with local resistance to the disruptive presence of a film crew, and other family friends helped out in various ways—the mother of one of the director's teenage pals let him do scenes in her apartment building at night and ended up with a cameo in the film, looking out the window just as she'd done when Scorsese was growing up.

TAXI DRIVER

Martin Scorsese (left) works through a *Taxi Driver* (1976) scene with Harvey Keitel (center) and Robert De Niro (right).

After going to the Southwest to shoot *Alice Doesn't Live Here Anymore* (1974), Scorsese came back to New York for *Taxi Driver* (1976), reuniting with Keitel and De Niro (who had become a major star thanks to *The Godfather, Part II*). De Niro earned another Academy Award nomination for his portrayal of Travis Bickle, an unbalanced Vietnam vet who nurtures twin obsessions over a teenage prostitute and a political candidate. The film was also nominated for best picture, and though it lost to *Rocky*, its success completed Scorsese's transformation from a promising young filmmaker to an accomplished director.

THAT'S ENTE

AMERICATHON

Before he created the *Police Academy* franchise in the mid-eighties, writer-director
Neal Israel gave us *Americathon* (1979), a delirious satire in which the United States
government holds a monthlong telethon to save itself from bankruptcy. Hosted by
Monty Rushmore (Harvey Korman, center), the telethon's musical guests included
Elvis Costello, Eddie Money, and the Del Rubio Triplets.

The next collaboration between Martin Scorsese and Robert De Niro after *Taxi Driver* was not quite as successful: reviewers were unenthusiastic about *New York, New York* (1977), and the audience followed their lead. (In all fairness to the director, however, the lavish production number intended to conclude the film was cut from the initial release, and when it was reinstated four years later, some critics revised their opinions upward.) Although he has come to be identified most readily as a director of crime dramas, Scorsese's decision to make a musical was not an entirely radical departure; in addition to growing up at movie theaters during the golden age of the MGM musical, he had, after all, earned his professional film-making chops by editing concert documentaries such as *Woodstock* (1970) and *Elvis on Tour* (1972).

PHANTOM OF THE PARADISE

Disfigured composer Winslow Leach swoops down to exact vengeance on those who have stolen his music in *Phantom of the Paradise* (1974). William Finley, who met director Brian De Palma when they were both students at Sarah Lawrence, appeared in many of the director's early films and helped create the design for his costume as the Phantom.

Scorsese was not the only filmmaker of his generation to experiment with the grandest of old-school genres. Francis Ford Coppola's full-fledged musicals, *Finian's Rainbow* and *One from the Heart*, were actually made before and after the 1970s, but he did manage to work some production numbers into *The Godfather, Part (II)*.

WATTSTAX

The daylong concert at Los Angeles Memorial Coliseum documented in *Wattstax* (1973) culminated in a performance by Isaac Hayes, but for years film audiences didn't get to hear his actual performance from that day because MGM refused to grant the filmmakers permission to use his live versions of "Theme from Shaft" and "Soulsville."

TOMMY

Ann-Margret was only three years older than Roger Daltrey when she played his mother in the rock opera *Tommy* (1975). The performance earned her a second Academy Award nomination.

Both Ted Neeley (left) and Carl Anderson had been in stage productions of *Jesus Christ Superstar* before they were cast as Jesus and Judas, respectively, in the film, but not together.

JESUS CHRIST SUPERSTAR

Peter Bogdanovich hung a plot on a collection of Cole Porter songs in *At Long Last Love* (1975), which had fared even worse than Scorsese's film. Brian De Palma had better luck with *Phantom of the Paradise* (1974), which gleefully satirized *The Phantom of the Opera*, the Faust legend, and most of the pop-music trends of the early part of the decade; the film's music, largely composed by Paul Williams, was nominated for an Academy Award. A year later, Keith Carradine would win the Oscar not for acting in Robert Altman's *Nashville*, but for penning the tune he sang in the movie, "I'm Easy." (Strictly speaking, of course, *Nashville* is not a musical, but a drama in which musical performances play a crucial role.)

HAIR

Treat Williams (center) stars as Berger, the charismatic hippie who serves as a guide to the counterculture in *Hair* (1979).

The musical genre would also be subject to other experiments and innovations during the decade. Ken Russell's 1975 adaptation of Pete Townshend's rock opera *Tommy* kept Who lead singer Roger Daltrey in the lead role but also incorporated other rock stars such as Eric Clapton and Elton John and required all the other actors, from Ann-Margret to Jack Nicholson, to sing their dialogue. Veteran director Norman Jewison took another concept album, Andrew Lloyd Webber and Tim Rice's *Jesus Christ Superstar*, and fleshed out its songs in the Israeli countryside; his movie and a cinematic version of the Broadway show *Godspell* were released only a few months apart in 1973. Original musicals were often crafted around literary works, from *Scrooge* (1970) to *Willy Wonka and the Chocolate Factory* (1971), although not all such films were as successful—the musical version of *Lost Horizon* (1973) was one of the film industry's most notorious failures. While songwriter Burt Bachrach's career wasn't hurt too badly by the flop, producer Ross Hunter never made another motion picture.

Although it would do so less and less as the decade progressed, Hollywood also continued to rely on Broadway as a source for suitable musicals, from *Fiddler on the Roof* (1971) to *Mame* (1974). Some shows took longer than others to make it from stage to screen: *1776* premiered on stage in 1969, a year after *Hair* made its Broadway debut, but the Founding Fathers were in movie theaters by 1972, while the hippies would have to wait until 1979, long after the war in Vietnam they had been protesting had ended.

Bob Fosse was able to move back and forth between Broadway and Hollywood effortlessly. By the time he began appearing in dance numbers in Hollywood musicals, he had already begun choreographing shows on Broadway. In 1969, he adapted his hit stage show *Sweet Charity*, which was itself a reworking of Federico Fellini's *Nights of Cabiria*, for the big screen. Although his next project, *Cabaret* (1972), had been directed by Harold Prince during its theatrical run, Fosse scrapped all the original choreography and made a film that was not just uniquely his own but one of the most critically acclaimed films of the decade. After doing the choreography for Stanley Donen's film version of *The Little Prince* (1974), Fosse ruthlessly mined his own life—specifically, the period where he was directing *Lenny* (1974) and putting together the Broadway musical *Chicago*—and transformed the raw material into *All That Jazz* (1979).

Just as Fosse was creating a film out of his own life, screenwriters Michael Cimino and Bo Goldman developed *The Rose* (1979) around Janis Joplin's biography. Other films would tell equally frank stories about creative artists without changing the names of those involved. Fosse's depiction of Lenny Bruce's drug addiction and rebellion against stifling conformity had been preceded by *Lady Sings the Blues* (1972), which offered a more conventional treatment of the life of Billie Holiday. Many of Ken Russell's films during the seventies addressed the challenges posed by the creative life, from *Savage Messiah* (1972) to *Valentino* (1977), although the lives of the sculptors, composers, and actors he chose as his subjects were often substantially altered when subject to his increasingly surreal cinematic vision.

That same vision resulted in *The Devils* (1971), loosely adapted from an Aldous Huxley book about an actual witch hunt in seventeenth-century France that is one of the most visually stunning historical dramas ever filmed. (The production designer was Derek Jarman, who was already making his own experimental short films and would begin applying his avant-garde sensibility to feature-length projects with

THE ROSE

Bette Midler's character in *The Rose* (1979) was openly modeled on the life of rock singer Janis Joplin, but the part was also tailored to Midler's strengths as a concert performer, which she had been honing in New York nightclubs throughout the decade. The theme song from the film also revitalized her recording career; it was her first hit single in eight years.

ALL THAT JAZZ

Roy Scheider and Ben Vereen are seen here in the "Bye Bye, Love" sequence, the big finale from *All That Jazz* (1979). The film's eclectic arrangement of the Everly Brothers tune was undoubtedly one of the prime considerations in the awarding of the Oscar for best musical score to Ralph Burns, who handled the music duties on all of Bob Fosse's films starting with *Sweet Charity* (1969).

LENNY

Dustin Hoffman was nominated for an Oscar for his starring role as Lenny Bruce in the 1974 biopic *Lenny*, which closed with Bruce's fatal overdose (above); two years earlier, Diana Ross earned similar accolades for her portrayal of another heroin addict, singer Billie Holiday, in *Lady Sings the Blues* (1972).

BOUND FOR GLORY

LEADBELLY

LADY SINGS THE BLUES

In 1976, Hal Ashby directed David Carradine in a film version of Woody Guthrie's autobiography, *Bound for Glory*, while Gordon Parks offered an African-American counterpoint with *Leadbelly*, starring Roger E. Mosley as Huddie Ledbetter. While the Guthrie biopic was nominated for best picture and would win Oscars for its score and cinematography, Parks's tribute to the groundbreaking blues musician has faded into obscurity.

KENTUCKY FRIED MOVIE

John Landis chases makeup artist Rick Baker (in the gorilla suit) on the set of *Kentucky Fried Movie* (1977), while writers David and Jerry Zucker look on. Landis had previously directed the horror-comedy *Schlock* (1973), but this was the first movie for the Zuckers, and a significant training ground for their next effort, *Airplane!* (1980).

HOLLYWOOD BOULEVARD

Dick Miller (left) as talent agent Walter Paisley in *Hollywood Boulevard* (1976). The character's name is a typical in-joke from codirector Joe Dante, referring to Miller's starring role in the 1959 Roger Corman film *A Bucket of Blood*.

THE DEVILS

Ken Russell's portrayal of sexual hysteria among the nuns of a seventeenth-century convent in *The Devils* (1971) made busy work for censors across Europe. It took three decades to recover footage from one lost scene in which the nuns have their way with a statue of Jesus.

BARRY LYNDON

THE FOUR MUSKETEERS

The lush romanticism of the historical costume drama was generally at odds with the gritty aesthetic of '70s Hollywood, but a few directors found ways to put their unique stamp on the genre. Stanley Kubrick's meticulous attention to period detail for *Barry Lyndon* (1975) was reflected in Oscar nods for art direction and costume design, while *The Three Musketeers* (1973) and its sequel turned swashbuckling into slapstick.

DIE RITTER
DER KOKOSNUSS
MONTY PYTHON AND THE
HOLY GRAIL

MONTY PYTHON AND THE HOLY GRAIL

After refilming some of their best television sketches for *And Now for Something Completely Different* (1971), British comedy troupe Monty Python turned to all-new material for two send-ups of the historical epic film. Terry Gilliam and Terry Jones shared directing duties on *Monty Python and the Holy Grail* (1975), while Jones directed *Life of Brian* (1979), the story of an inadvertent false messiah in the time of Jesus, on his own.

Sebastiane in 1976.) Among the handful of costume dramas from the period that can compare to it in intensity are Roman Polanski's gory *Macbeth* (also 1971) and Stanley Kubrick's *Barry Lyndon* (1975), a poised adaptation of William Makepeace Thackeray's novel. Some critics might also include *Caligula* (1979), for which producer Bob Guccione hired the most prestigious cast ever to appear in a hard-core sex movie, but almost everybody involved with the project—including Malcolm McDowell, who starred as the insane Roman emperor—would later express regret at their participation.

Richard Lester originally conceived of *The Three Musketeers* (1973) as a vehicle for the Beatles, with whom he had collaborated on *A Hard Day's Night* (1964) and *Help!* (1965). After the band broke up, he retooled the concept and, with the help of screenwriter George

ULTRA-COOL ACTOR
RAQUEL WELCH

"My purpose in coming to Hollywood is the destruction of the American male in all its particulars."

After divorcing her first husband, James Welch, in 1964, Jo Raquel Tejada kept his name and with the help of her second spouse, actor-turned-publicist Patrick Curtis, she set out on an acting career. The decision wasn't as radical as Margarita Cansino's acceptance of an overhauled identity as Rita Hayworth, but it achieved the same effect, smoothing out her ethnic background to pitch her sex appeal to as broad a segment of America's film audiences as possible. A string of films throughout the late sixties—from *Fantastic Voyage* and *One Million Years B.C.* (both 1966) to *100 Rifles* (1969)—made her a star, but her first film in the 1970s, *Myra Breckinridge*, was a major setback to her ambitions.

Critics and audiences found much of *Myra* incoherent, and what they could understand they found offensive. (Gore Vidal, who wrote the satirical tale of a male-to-female transsexual who seeks to undermine Hollywood from within, vocally disowned the film.) Welch worked on rebuilding her star power by picking more traditional screen fare, such as the feminist revenge western *Hannie Caulder* (1971) and the ensemble police procedural *Fuzz* (1972). But there was a critical difference in her post-*Myra* career; although she would still play sexy, she wasn't exactly a sex kitten anymore. Her roles in the seventies carried more substance and often recast her as a working-class heroine. In *Kansas City Bomber* (1972), she's a single mom who supports her kids by playing in competitive roller-derby leagues; in *Mother, Jugs, and Speed* (1976), she's an ambulance dispatcher with ambitions of becoming a paramedic.

Even when Welch did take on more glamorous parts in costume dramas such as *The Three Musketeers* (1973) and *Crossed Swords* (1978), the films—and her performances—were shot through with an air of self-mockery. Her film career tapered off in the late seventies, but stage and television gigs have kept her active into the twenty-first century.

MYRA BRECKINRIDGE

MacDonald Fraser, created a sprawling, swashbuckling, comic epic with an all-star cast ranging from Michael York as D'Artagnan to Charlton Heston as Cardinal Richelieu. The film was so huge that it eventually became two films, with *The Four Musketeers* (1974) picking up the second half of the story. Several of the actors involved sued, believing they should be paid the equivalent of two films' salaries, although some cast members, including Oliver Reed and Raquel Welch, would reunite with producer Ilya Salkind for *Crossed Swords* (1978).

Lester followed his Musketeers films with two more subversive swashbucklers: *Royal Flash* (1975), an adaptation of one of Fraser's bestselling *Flashman* novels; and *Robin and Marian* (1976), which cast Sean Connery and Audrey Hepburn as Sherwood Forest's famous couple in their golden years. As filming for *Robin and Marian* began, in May 1975, Connery's fans could see him in theaters as the dashing Berber pirate el-Raisuli the Magnificent in John Milius's *The Wind and the Lion*, and he would pop up again a few months later with Michael Caine in *The Man Who Would Be King*. John Huston's version of the Rudyard Kipling tale earned four Oscar nominations, including one for best adapted screenplay—solid vindication for a film Huston had spent nearly two decades trying to make.

SILENT MOVIE

Bernadette Peters as seductress Vilma Kaplan, who tries to stop director Mel Fun (Mel Brooks, flanked by Marty Feldman and Dom DeLuise) from saving Big Picture Studios with his comeback film in *Silent Movie* (1976).

SATURDAY NIGHT FEVER

John Travolta shows off his moves in a series of photographs from *Saturday Night Fever* (1977). Paramount released the film in late 1977 with an R rating but it was then recut to a PG version to capitalize on Travolta's massive popularity with teenage girls.

SGT. PEPPERS LONELY HEARTS CLUB BAND

Sgt. Pepper's Lonely Hearts Club Band (1978) starred Peter Frampton (second from left) and the Bee Gees making their way through a flimsy plot constructed around as many Beatles songs as the producers could acquire the rights to; supporting characters were also drawn from the songs, including George Burns (center) as Mr. Kite.

THE ROCKY HORROR PICTURE SHOW

Tim Curry, in full Dr. Frank-N-Furter drag, takes a break on the set of *The Rocky Horror Picture Show* (1975). Behind him, dressed as Riff Raff, is costar Richard O'Brien, who cowrote the original stage show with director Jim Sharman.

QUADROPHENIA

The role of Ace, a bad influence on young Mods in *Quadrophenia* (1979), was Sting's first experience in film.

THE WIZ

The Wiz (1978) reimagined *The Wizard of Oz* (1939) with an African-American focus, starring Diana Ross as a young schoolteacher named Dorothy making her way through an urban-tinged Oz. Her companions included (from left to right) Michael Jackson as the Scarecrow, Nipsey Russell as the Tinman, and Ted Ross as the Cowardly Lion.

THANK GOD IT'S FRIDAY

Although the film failed to catch on at the box office, Donna Summer's showstopping "Last Dance" won the Oscar for best song. Ray Vitte as Bobby Speed, the DJ at the disco where *Thank God It's Friday* (1978) takes place.

GIMME SHELTER

The Hell's Angels provided aggressively violent security for the free concert at Altamont documented in *Gimme Shelter* (1970). One concertgoer was stabbed to death in front of the stage later in the evening; the gang member charged with the killing was acquitted on grounds of self-defense when footage revealed that the victim had pulled a gun first.

THE LAST WALTZ

Joni Mitchell, Neil Young, and Bob Dylan were among the performers who joined the Band for their farewell concert as captured by Martin Scorsese's *The Last Waltz* (1976).

THE SONG REMAINS THE SAME

The members of Led Zeppelin didn't particularly like the footage from their live shows at Madison Square Garden at the end of the "Houses of the Holy" tour, but they were contractually obliged to release a concert film, so *The Song Remains the Same* (1976) also includes a fantasy sequence starring each member of the band, including Robert Plant's rescue of a maiden trapped in a castle.

NASHVILLE

Although he comes from a prominent acting family, Keith Carradine is the only member of the clan to have won the Academy Award—and it was for songwriting. After composing and singing "I'm Easy" in *Nashville* (1975), Carradine also sang in Alan Rudolph's 1977 film *Welcome to L.A.* and in the 1990s was nominated for a Tony for his performance in the Broadway musical *The Will Rogers Follies*.

WILLIE WONKA AND THE CHOCOLATE FACTORY

Gene Wilder plays the reclusive candy man in *Willie Wonka and the Chocolate Factory* (1971). Director Mel Stuart's children handed him Roald Dahl's novel and insisted he turn it into a movie; both children would make small cameos in the film.

ULTRA-COOL ACTOR
LIZA MINNELLI

"Life is a cabaret, old chum."

"Life is a cabaret, old chum."

Liza Minnelli was little more than a year old when she made her film debut in *In the Good Old Summertime* (1949), "playing" the infant child of her real-life mother, Judy Garland; the film was directed by her father, Vincente Minnelli. Her real career began in earnest in the 1960s, when she began appearing on the New York stage and in concert. After winning the Tony Award when she was only nineteen, she soon shifted over to motion pictures and was nominated for the best supporting actress Oscar for her performance in *The Sterile Cuckoo* (1969).

She followed that auspicious debut with the title role in *Tell Me You Love Me, Junie Moon* (1970) and then took the part of Sally Bowles in the film adaptation of the hit Broadway show *Cabaret*. The film won eight of the ten Academy Awards for which it was nominated, including a best-actress award for Minnelli. Subsequent film roles would make use of her dual talents as a singer and an actress, usually with the assistance of *Cabaret* composer John Kander and Fred Ebb, who provided tunes for *Lucky Lady* (1975) and *New York, New York* (1977). The theme from the latter movie would take on a life of its own, becoming a signature song not just for Minnelli, but for Frank Sinatra (and, in the 1983 animated short *Sundae in New York*, then-mayor Ed Koch). They also wrote songs for the only other film Liza made with her father, *A Matter of Time* (1976), which flopped at theaters after the producers recut the film to suit their own interests.
.

CABARET

Other attempts to jump on the adventure-film bandwagon were not so successful. At the peak of his fame, Robert Shaw captained a motley crew of pirates ranging from James Earl Jones to Avery Schreiber in *Swashbuckler* (1976), but even he was powerless to keep the film from sinking. Beau Bridges, saddled with the role of a foppish British officer in that film, would fare little better in *The 5th Musketeer* (1979), playing the dual roles of Louis XIV and his secret twin brother, who happens to be the protégé of the aging Musketeers: José Ferrer, Lloyd Bridges, and Alan Hale Jr. The film also features European erotica starlet Sylvia Kristel in her first major English-language performance, making her way awkwardly through sex scenes rather timidly staged in comparison to *Emmanuelle* (1974) and its sequels.

O LUCKY MAN!

Malcolm McDowell reprised the role of Michael Travis, the rebellious student from *If . . .* (1968) in Lindsay Anderson's *O Lucky Man!* (1973). His satirical journey through the corrupt modern-day world is periodically interrupted by self-referential cinematic techniques and several tunes sung by pop star Alan Price (a former member of the Animals).

CHARACTER

Woody Allen directs Jonathan Munk, who played the young Alvy Singer in *Annie Hall* (1977). It was Munk's only film role; three years later his brother Robert played the Allen stand-in in *Stardust Memories*.

STUDIES

CARNAL KNOWLEDGE

One of documentary photographer Mary Ellen Mark's first jobs was shooting production stills for Hollywood pictures, including *Carnal Knowledge* (1971). She took this photograph of Jack Nicholson, as well as the iconic portrait of Ann-Margret he's carrying.

For film audiences of the 1970s, New York City was often a symbol of urban anarchy, a place where muggers freely roamed the streets and, according to *The Taking of Pelham One Two Three* (1974), the subways. The prevalence of crime in Manhattan was so widely recognized that Woody Allen was able to mine it repeatedly for laughs, whether setting himself up for a subway holdup in *Bananas* (1971) or having *Annie Hall* costar Tony Roberts toss off a one-liner about being mugged while performing Shakespeare in Central Park.

ANNIE HALL

Annie Hall costars Woody Allen, Diane Keaton, and Tony Roberts emerge from below a Manhattan sidewalk, accompanied by the film's coauthor Marshall Brickman.

Allen could kid New York City with impunity, though, because deep down he clearly loved his hometown. He was, in some ways, a quintessential cinematic New Yorker: the bundle of nervous energy from Brooklyn who can't quite believe he's made it into Manhattan. New York was a constant backdrop in his movies during the 1970s, as it has been throughout his career; in films such as *Annie Hall* (1977) and *Manhattan* (1979), one might even say the city rises to the level of a secondary character, and protagonists who stray outside the city limits—whether they wind up in Central American revolutions (*Bananas*) or futuristic dystopias (*Sleeper*, 1973)—remain variations on Allen's comic persona of intellectual confidence matched only by emotional insecurity. Even Boris Grushenko, the nineteenth-century

Russian protagonist of *Love and Death* (1975), is really an anachronistic nebbish whose period costuming just provides him more opportunities to fire off some zingers.

After *Annie Hall* won Academy Awards for best picture, best director, and best screenplay, Allen briefly took himself out of the equation in *Interiors* (1978), the first of his films in which he did not appear. The Ingmar Bergman–influenced drama retained some of the existentialist humor of Allen's previous films, but scenes that would have been played for laughs earlier in the decade were now occasions for raw emotional trauma. When he reappeared in front of the camera in *Manhattan*, some of the comedy returned with him, although it was clear now that Allen's dramatic concerns were more than a passing phase, leading many viewers to register complaints the director would slyly acknowledge in *Stardust Memories* (1980) when visiting aliens tell Allen they prefer his "earlier, funnier films."

"YOU'RE A FUNNY MAN, AL. A PAIN IN THE ASS BUT A FUNNY MAN"

Woody Allen was one of three Brooklynites who emerged from the writing staff of Sid Caesar's *Your Show of Shows* and began directing movies in the late 1960s, then truly came into their own the following decade. Mel Brooks became a master of movie parody; *Blazing Saddles* and *Young Frankenstein* were released just eleven months apart, in 1974, followed in quick succession by *Silent Movie* (1976) and *High Anxiety* (1977). Carl Reiner began the seventies by directing George Segal in the darkly comedic *Where's Poppa?* (1970), went on to solidify the public persona of George Burns with *Oh, God!* (1977), and then helped launch Steve Martin's film career with *The Jerk* (1979).

Fellow writer Neil Simon, like his three coworkers, also grew up in Brooklyn, and although he didn't become a director, he would wield significant influence over seventies screen comedy as a playwright who would adapt his own material for the movies, describing New Yorkers in midlife crisis in *Last of the Red Hot Lovers* (1972) and *The Prisoner of Second Avenue* (1975). He turned blatantly autobiographical with *Chapter Two* (1979), starring his actual second wife, Marsha Mason, as the woman the widowed protagonist falls in love with and weds. Simon also wrote several original screenplays during this period, including a pair of mystery spoofs directed by Robert Moore, *Murder by Death* (1976) and *The Cheap Detective* (1978).

THE OUT-OF-TOWNERS

PLAZA SUITE

THE PRISONER OF SECOND AVENUE

KOTCH

THE GOODBYE GIRL

Although Neil Simon, Jack Lemmon, and Walter Matthau worked together in complete unison only on *The Odd Couple* (1968) and its eventual sequel, they frequently paired off with each other in the 1970s. Simon originally conceived the married couple played by Lemmon and Sandy Dennis in *The Out-of-Towners* (1970) for one of the story lines in his play *Plaza Suite* (1971) but eventually took them aside and expanded their urban adventure to the point where it needed to be a movie. Lemmon would also star in the film version of *The Prisoner of Second Avenue* (1975), and when *Plaza Suite* found its way to the big screen, Matthau (seen chatting with Simon) played all three male leads. Matthau also starred in Lemmon's one film as a director, *Kotch* (1971), in which the fifty-year-old actor made himself up to play a man twenty years older. Another Simon regular was his second wife, Marsha Mason, who earned three of her four Oscar nominations for roles created for her by Simon, including 1977's *The Goodbye Girl* (left, with Richard Dreyfuss and Quinn Cummings).

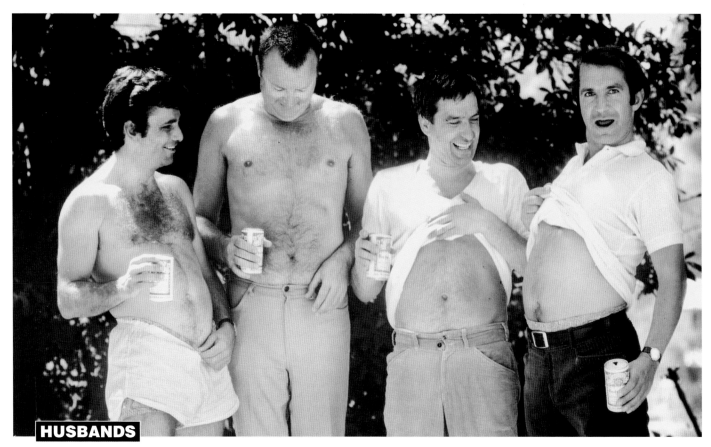

HUSBANDS

John Cassavetes (above, second from right) used the money he made acting in Hollywood films to finance independent productions such as *Husbands* (1970) and *Minnie and Moskowitz* (1971), working with a core group of actors and film professionals from one production to the next. His wife, Gena Rowlands, earned an Oscar nomination as the mad housewife in *A Woman Under the Influence* (1974), while close friend Ben Gazzara starred in *The Killing of a Chinese Bookie* (1976), a rare detour for Cassavetes into the crime genre. Peter Falk was also a regular member of the Cassavetes troupe, and the two collaborated on other projects as well, including their roles as two friends whose relationship is strained by their organized-crime ties in Elaine May's *Mikey & NIcky* (1976).

THE KILLING OF A CHINESE BOOKIE

A WOMAN UNDER THE INFLUENCE

MINNIE AND MOSKOWITZ

MIKEY & NICKY

NEXT STOP, GREENWICH VILLAGE

The cast of **Next Stop, Greenwich Village** (1976) poses together on a New York stoop. Writer-director Paul Mazursky based the character of Larry Lipinsky (Lenny Baker, top left) on his own arrival in the Village in the early 1950s. Although the rest of the gang—Antonio Fargas, Dori Brenner, Lois Smith, and Christopher Walken—continued to work in film, Baker went to Broadway and won a Tony for his part in the musical *I Love My Wife*.

The director who worked most closely with Simon over the years, including on the hits *The Sunshine Boys* (1975) and *The Goodbye Girl* (1977), was Herbert Ross, a former ballet dancer who got his start in Hollywood choreographing movie musicals such as *Inside Daisy Clover* (1965). He began directing in 1969 with a musical remake of *Goodbye, Mister Chips*, and although he would occasionally draw upon his background for films such as *The Turning Point* (1977), he did only one musical during the seventies. (That film, the Fanny Brice biopic *Funny Lady* [1975], starred another of his frequent collaborators, Barbra Streisand, whose 1968 film debut as Brice in *Funny Girl* he choreographed.) Although he was often labeled a "woman's director," he was equally adept at handling actors, from Woody Allen (*Play It Again, Sam*, 1972) to Robert Duvall and Laurence Olivier (*The Seven-Per-Cent Solution*, 1976).

"I'M ALL DRESSED UP AND READY TO FALL IN LOVE!"

Many other directors adopted New York City as a setting for their dramas, frequently touching upon social issues that affected the lives of all Americans. For his American filmmaking debut, Milos Forman poked fun at the generation gap with *Taking Off* (1971), and baby boomers enduring strained relations with their parents might also have identified with the slightly older Gene Hackman and his dilemma in *I Never Sang for My Father*

HAROLD AND MAUDE

Bud Cort and Ruth Gordon wait on the set of *Harold and Maude* (1971). Bad reviews drove the film out of theaters almost instantly, but the film has become a cult classic, the most recognized work by either star or by director Hal Ashby.

SHAMPOO

When Robert Towne began writing *Shampoo* (1975) in the late sixties, he turned to his real stylist, Jay Sebring, as inspiration for the character eventually played by Warren Beatty (who also got his hair cut by Sebring). Towne took nearly a decade to complete the script; in the interim, Sebring had become one of the victims of Charlie Manson and his disciples.

THE SEDUCTION OF JOE TYNAN

Meryl Streep hit the acting jackpot costarring with Dustin Hoffman in *Kramer vs. Kramer,* Woody Allen in *Manhattan,* and Alan Alda in *The Seduction of Joe Tynan*. She won the best supporting actress Oscar for *Kramer* after beating out Kate Jackson and Jane Fonda for the part and rewriting her own dialogue for the courtroom scene with encouragement from writer-director Robert Benton.

ALICE DOESN'T LIVE HERE ANYMORE

As the effects of women's liberation and the sexual revolution spread throughout society, Hollywood films began to reflect the changing lives of American women. Ellen Burstyn (with Kris Kristofferson, right) plays a widowed mom struggling to make ends meet as a waitress in Martin Scorsese's *Alice Doesn't Live Here Anymore* (1974), the source for Linda Lavin's hit sitcom *Alice*. As the title character of *An Unmarried Woman* (1978), Jill Clayburgh navigates her way through life after divorce, while Diane Keaton (with costar Richard Gere) discovers the less savory side of the singles scene in *Looking for Mr. Goodbar* (1977).

AN UNMARRIED WOMAN

LOOKING FOR MR. GOODBAR

(1970). Urban families struggling to make ends meet could relate to Diahann Carroll's plight in *Claudine* (1974), as her character tries to raise several children alone and start a new romantic relationship while negotiating her way through the red tape of the welfare system. *Carnal Knowledge* (1971) to *Looking for Mr. Goodbar* (1977) offer dark-tinged commentary on changing sexual mores, while films such as *Kramer vs. Kramer* and *Rich Kids* (both 1979) address the growing divorce rate and its impact on families.

The sexual revolution could hardly be confined to New York City, of course. Russ Meyer had pioneered the sexploitation film in the 1960s, and when Hollywood studios were able to treat sexuality with the same frankness he had shown in his independent movies, 20th Century Fox hired him for a three-picture deal that began with *Beyond the Valley of the Dolls* (1970). The next year, he turned in an adaptation of Irving Wallace's *The Seven Minutes*, but after the drama about a bookseller facing obscenity charges for selling an erotic novel flopped, Meyer returned to his independent filmmaking roots just as another maverick director, Baltimore's John Waters, began making a name for himself with underground hits like *Pink Flamingos* (1972) and *Female Trouble* (1974).

The loosening of culture attitudes toward sexuality also brought about public acknowledgment and (limited) acceptance of hard-core and soft-core

THE BOYS IN THE BAND

Although William Friedkin would eventually specialize in suspense films, his early movies displayed a range of comedic and dramatic subject matter. *The Boys in the Band* (1970), adapted by Matt Crowley from his own hit play, was one of the first films with protagonists whose homosexuality was not somehow coded or obscured.

ONE FLEW OVER THE CUCKOO'S NEST

One Flew Over the Cuckoo's Nest (1975) was filmed on location at a mental hospital in Oregon, and the actual patients interacted regularly with the cast and crew, appearing in the film as extras or working as technical assistants. In addition to Jack Nicholson, who won the Oscar for best actor, the film costarred (from left) Delos V. Smith Jr., Will Sampson, Brad Dourif (nominated for best supporting actor), Danny DeVito, and William Redfield.

WHERE'S POPPA?

George Segal plays the once-dutiful son who now hopes to speed his crazy mother (Ruth Gordon) into the grave so he can get on with his life in *Where's Poppa?* (1970).

EVERYTHING YOU ALWAYS WANTED TO KNOW ABOUT SEX...BUT WERE AFRAID TO ASK

Woody Allen allegedly based *Everything You Always Wanted to Know About Sex . . . But Were Afraid to Ask* (1972) on a best-selling nonfiction book by Dr. David Reuben; but skits such as Gene Wilder's fling with bestiality had a tenuous connection, at best, to the real contents of the popular sex manual.

LAST TANGO IN PARIS

Marlon Brando and Maria Schneider acted out Bernardo Bertolucci's sexual fantasies in *Last Tango in Paris* (1972) with such power that the film and its stars were put on trial for obscenity in Italy. Brando was so emotionally drained by the role, which entailed elaborate improvisation, that he did not speak to the director for more than a decade.

BEHIND THE GREEN DOOR

When Marilyn Chambers starred in *Behind the Green Door* (1972), she became one of the most famous actresses in the country. The role was a long way from her film debut in Barbra Streisand's *The Owl and the Pussycat* (1971).

ULTRA-COOL ACTOR
WALTER MATTHAU

> "We've had nice talking, now we're going to have door breaking."

The 1970s began late for Walter Matthau, but when *A New Leaf* opened in March 1971, his starring role as an amoral (and bankrupt) schemer out to marry and murder a scatterbrained heiress kicked off a string of performances that would make any actor proud. Two months later, he could be seen in three separate roles in the film version of Neil Simon's *Plaza Suite*, and in the fall, he got his second Academy Award nomination, for *Kotch*, a film directed by his close friend and colleague Jack Lemmon.

Pete 'n' Tillie (1972) offered further evidence of Matthau's flair for offbeat comedies, but in *Charley Verrick* (1973), he was a bank robber on the run from the mob, while *The Laughing Policeman* (1973) and *The Taking of Pelham One Two Three* (1974) cast him as weary but dedicated law enforcement officers in San Francisco and New York City, respectively. A reluctant cameo role as a wisecracking barfly in *Earthquake* (1974) followed, but when the actor saw how his scenes had been edited to make it appear as if he was a costar, he got his revenge by ordering them to list his credit under a phony "birth name," Matuschanskayasky.

After that, he reunited with Lemmon and director Billy Wilder for a lighthearted remake of *The Front Page* (1974) and then another Neil Simon part (and another Oscar nomination) in *The Sunshine Boys* (1975). *The Bad News Bears* (1976) and *Casey's Shadow* (1978) added new facets to his curmudgeonly persona, while *House Calls* (also 1978) revisited familiar romantic-comedy territory. His work during the decade ended as it had begun, with three films in a single year, one of them from a Neil Simon script; to make the coincidence even more meaningful, 1978's *California Suite* is practically a mirror image of *Plaza Suite*, substituting the Beverly Hills Hotel for the Plaza.

THE TAKING OF PELHAM 1, 2, 3

pornographic films as a cultural phenomenon. *Deep Throat* and *Behind the Green Door* (both 1972) were box-office hits, leading to other successes such as *The Devil in Miss Jones* (1973), *The Opening of Misty Beethoven* (1976), and *Emmanuelle* (1974). Mainstream films, too, would discuss sexuality more frankly, so much so that when Bernardo Bertolucci's *Last Tango in Paris* came out in 1972, some viewers thought it downright pornographic.

Although it would be a long time before they would find widespread social acceptance, and homophobia would be a constant source of cinematic humor throughout the decade, gay men could at least begin to see themselves portrayed with open sympathy in films such as *The Boys in the Band* (1970), *Sunday, Bloody Sunday* (1971), and *Butley* (1976). Fabulously queer characters also provided comic relief in *The Rocky Horror Picture Show* (1975) and the French import *La Cage aux Folles* (1978) . . . and then there was *A Different Story* (also 1978), a romantic comedy where a gay man and lesbian marry so he can stay in the country. It was pretty much the only decent lesbian role of the decade in an American film—almost all the others were either vampires or gratuitous sex performers—and she winds up falling in love with the guy.

SUNDAY, BLOODY SUNDAY

After shooting *Midnight Cowboy* (1969) in America and winning Oscars for best picture and best director, John Schlesinger (right) returned to England to direct *Sunday, Bloody Sunday* (1971), with Glenda Jackson as the young woman who shares her boyfriend with another man. The script was written by Penelope Gilliatt, a London-based film critic who shared reviewing duties at the *New Yorker* with Pauline Kael.

LIFE OUTSIDE

THE STEPFORD WIVES

The women of Stepford go shopping in one of the most iconic images from the original version of *The Stepford Wives* (1975). The fancy dresses and floppy hats were a late touch: William Goldman's original draft of the screenplay called for the women to wear miniskirts.

THE BIG CITY

The cast of Peter Bogdanovich's *The Last Picture Show* (1971) were almost entirely unknown actors who had been in few, if any, films beforehand. That was the way the director wanted it, hoping that the absence of movie stars would keep the audience's attention focused on the stories taking place in Anarene, Texas. The one exception to the rule was veteran character-actor Ben Johnson in the role of Sam the Lion, the closest thing this small town had to a patriarch in the early 1950s—and Johnson had strongly resisted the offer, even after Bogdanovich asked fellow director John Ford to intercede on

CRAZY MAMA

Ann Sothern takes aim while Cloris Leachman covers her back in a scene from *Crazy Mama* (1975). Jonathan Demme stepped in to direct the film at Roger Corman's request after the original director dropped out.

his behalf. Although Bogdanovich went out to Nashville to interview several country musicians as possible candidates for the part while he was studying the music that would be heard throughout the film, he was determined to cast Johnson, and his persistence ultimately paid off. The results speak for themselves— the film, shot for just over a million dollars, became one of the year's top-ten hits, and of its eight Academy Award nominations, its two victories were in the acting categories: best supporting actress for Cloris Leachman and best supporting actor for Johnson.

THE LAST PICTURE SHOW

When *The Last Picture Show* opened in late 1971, Timothy Bottoms had done only one other

film, *Johnny Got His Gun* (1971), and while Cloris Leachman had been acting since the 1950s, she

was—until she won the Oscar—best known as a comic foil on *The Mary Tyler Moore Show*.

Although he did plenty of research for the film, and worked extensively with novelist Larry McMurtry on the screenplay, native New Yorker Bogdanovich's emotional connection to Anarene by necessity had a degree of remove. George Lucas, on the other hand, had a very intimate connection with the material in *American Graffiti* (1973), set in the early sixties small-town California where he himself had come of age. The two films diverge in many ways, but take fundamentally common approaches; both are low-budget efforts, populated by an ensemble cast of then-emerging talent acting out the rituals of teen sexuality while the music of the period plays from every radio, jukebox, or band in the vicinity. But while Bogdanovich won nearly instant approval when he turned in his finished film to BBS, executives at Universal hated what Lucas delivered to them—it wasn't until Francis Ford Coppola, who had handled producing duties for Lucas, offered to buy the film back that they agreed to release it.

Although set in 1962, *Graffiti* became the prime instigator of a wave of nostalgia concentrated primarily on the 1950s and the birth of rock 'n' roll. The television series *Happy Days* was the most obvious manifestation of this nostalgia, but movies such as *The Lords of Flatbush* (1974), *September 30, 1955* (1977), and *The Buddy Holly Story* (1978) would also

AMERICAN GRAFFITI

Although Richard Dreyfuss had been acting in films since the late sixties, *American Graffiti* (1973) was his first prominent role. He would get lead parts in subsequent films, but it would be a few more years before he rose to genuine stardom, beginning with his performance in *Jaws* (1975).

HARPER VALLEY P.T.A.

One of the handful of films based on hit songs, *Harper Valley P.T.A.* (1978) is probably the most successful. Country singer Bobbie Gentry's attack on small-town hypocrisy became the basis for a comedy starring Barbara Eden (standing) as a liberated mother who takes farcical revenge against local bluenoses.

SOUNDER

Although Paul Winfield (being handcuffed) was nominated as best actor for his role in *Sounder* (1972), some might argue that the film really belongs to Kevin Hooks (kneeling), making his acting debut as a young boy in Depression-era Louisiana. Hooks is now an accomplished film and television director, and revisited this story for a 2003 remake.

DELIVERANCE

Ned Beatty, Jon Voigt, Ronnie Cox (being carried), and Burt Reynolds are seen here as the weekend outdoorsmen forced to fight for their survival in *Deliverance* (1972). The film was shot on location with the actors doing the majority of their own stunts, which was why Marlon Brando, Jimmy Stewart, and Henry Fonda all turned down the role that eventually went to Reynolds, who wound up injuring himself going over a waterfall.

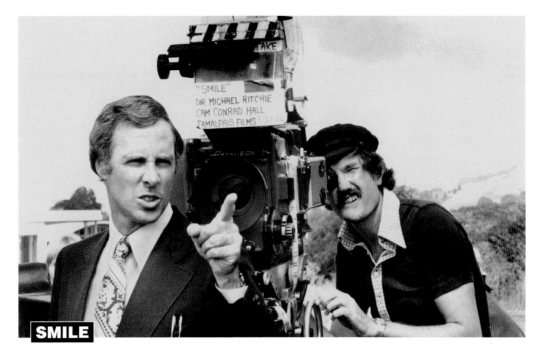

SMILE

Michael Ritchie (right) directs Bruce Dern in *Smile* (1975), a satire about the effect of a beauty pageant on a small California community. Ritchie's films in the seventies often centered around the theme of competition, from tapping a political underdog in *The Candidate* (1972) to the down-and-dirty athletes of *Semi-Tough* (1977) and *The Bad News Bears* (1976).

benefit from the long-term effects of *Graffiti*'s popularity. Universal would even try to strike gold (without Lucas) by bringing several cast members back for *More American Graffiti* in 1979, while the team of Robert Zemeckis and Bob Gale made their Hollywood debut by looking back at Beatlemania in *I Want to Hold Your Hand* (1978). Other films openly mocked or subverted the *Graffiti* model, especially the end titles revealing the characters' ultimate fates: *Cooley High* (1975) looks back at the same era from an African-American perspective while National Lampoon's *Animal House* turns its wrap-up into a string of one-liners, where the ROTC leader is "killed in Vietnam by his own troops" and drunken Bluto becomes a U.S. senator.

American filmmakers also frequently revisited the earlier half of the twentieth century. Peter Bogdanovich's *Paper Moon* (1973) is one of the most notable examples. *Ace Eli and Rodger of the Skies*, which uses a similar father-child dynamic to tell the story of a barnstorming pilot and his son, beat *Paper Moon* into the theaters by a month, but Ryan and Tatum O'Neal quickly trumped Cliff Robertson and Eric Shea. The 1930s were especially popular, still riding the

GREASE

Jeff Conaway, Olivia Newton-John, John Travolta, and Stockard Channing get out of high school in the finale of *Grease* (1978). Conaway, in the role of Travolta's sidekick, had to slouch while performing to make the star look taller; as a further indignity, his character's one song ("Greased Lightning") was reassigned to Travolta.

ROCK 'N' ROLL HIGH SCHOOL

P. J. Soles dances with the Ramones down the halls of *Rock 'n' Roll High School* (1979). The band was paid just $5,000 for their performance and was hired only after Cheap Trick and Tom Petty and the Heartbreakers turned down the film.

ULTRA-COOL ACTOR BURT REYNOLDS

"You want me to drive to Texarkana, pick up four hundred cases of Coors, and come back in twenty-eight hours? No problem."

Burt Reynolds was born in Georgia and moved to Florida when he was still in school. After more than a decade of television and movie westerns, he barreled his way into stardom in 1972 as the expedition leader with the survivalist skills to pull his buddies through the weekend from hell in *Deliverance*. He began to play up his Southern roots in films such as *White Lightning* (1973), *W. W. and the Dixie Dancekings* (1975), and *Gator* (1976) but also kept one foot in the urban-crime genre, playing a cop in *Fuzz* (1972) and a private eye in *Shamus* (1973). He also dabbled with period pieces, although those films, including the musicals *At Long Last Love* and *Lucky Lady* (both 1975), failed to entice audiences the way his good ol' boy act did.

One of his closest friends in the industry was Hal Needham, his stunt double on the TV series *Gunsmoke*. As Reynolds began to acquire more clout in the industry, he did his best to make room for Needham on his film projects beyond the stunt-coordinating role he had played on westerns throughout the sixties. After performing second-unit work on *White Lightning*, *The Longest Yard* (1974), and *Gator*, Needham came to Reynolds with an idea for a story that played off his *White Lightning* moonshine driver persona. Reynolds liked the concept behind *Smokey and the Bandit* so much that he made sure Needham got the director's job as well, and the result was the second-highest grossing film of 1977 . . . about $100 million or so behind *Star Wars*.

THE MAN WHO LOVED CAT DANCING

PINK FLAMINGOS

Divine, seen here in her breakthrough role as Babs Johnson, "the filthiest woman alive," was a regular participant in John Waters's movies. The three-hundred-pound transvestite was a former high-school classmate of Waters and was willing to go to any length for his favorite director—including the infamous climax of *Pink Flamingos* (1972).

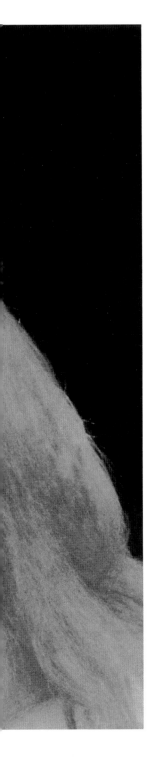

boost *Bonnie and Clyde* had given the period crime film in the late sixties, and although moon-shiners and bootlegging drivers were hardly innovative cinematic antiheroes in the 1970s, the sheer proliferation of films about them during this period bears noting. Films from *The Moonshine War* (1970) to *Big Bad Mama* (1974) are set in or around the Prohibition era, but many others, such as *White Lightning* (1973) or *Moonshine County Express* (1977), depict the illicit activities as continuing to the present day. These films were almost always shot heavily on location in Southern states, partly for the sake of realism, but also because the labor costs on regionally made films could be significantly lower than those for films shot in New York or Los Angeles.

Particularly as African-American actors became more prominent on-screen, films set in the South continued to deal directly with racism — or, as in the case of 1975's *Mandingo*, exploit it rather shamelessly. The movie . . . *tick* . . . *tick* . . . *tick* . . . (1970) pits a newly elected black sheriff against his community's white residents, a *Blazing Saddles* situation unfolding without the humor. The New Orleans radio station at the heart of *WUSA* (also 1970) is a hotbed of rabid, race-baiting conservatism, not that far removed from the KKK. The Klan put in an actual appearance in the 1974 bomb *The Klansman*, which is memorable chiefly for being O. J. Simpson's first movie; that same year, a number of other African-American football players starred in *The Black Six* as a gang who fight back when the brother of one of the bikers is murdered for dating a white girl.

The class struggle was also a frequent source for stories set outside the major urban centers. *Fighting Mad* (1976), the last of three films Jonathan Demme directed for Roger Corman, follows a man back to his family's ranch in Arkansas, where he gets caught up in a battle between the rural community and a strip-mining corporation, in which the family's refusal to sell their land leads to the usual escalated violence: the younger brother and his pregnant wife are murdered by hired thugs, and pretty soon the working-class hero is blowing up bulldozers and loading his crossbow. The script is so saturated with corruption that the evil mining executive is not

ULTRA-COOL ACTOR
BARBRA STREISAND

"Love, soft as an easy chair."

After conquering Broadway and television in the 1960s, Barbra Streisand set her sights on Hollywood, beginning with the transferral of her Tony-nominated performance in *Funny Girl* to the big screen in 1968. The film earned her an Oscar for best actress and was quickly followed by two more musicals, *Hello Dolly!* (1969) and *On a Clear Day You Can See Forever* (1970). Eager to prove her dramatic chops, she began choosing parts that didn't require her to sing and quickly found a niche for herself in romantic comedy. After teaming with George Segal in *The Owl and the Pussycat* (1970), she voiced strong reservations about Peter Bogdanovich's *What's Up, Doc?* and continued to predict its failure even after accepting the lead. It went on to become one of the biggest hits of 1972 and her most successful film of the decade.

Combining Streisand's box-office clout with Robert Redford's made the romantic melodrama *The Way We Were* (1973) a hit, too, albeit on a smaller scale. Streisand was nominated for a second Academy Award and also sang the film's Oscar-winning theme song. She returned to the role of Fanny Brice for *Funny Lady,* a 1975 sequel made under litigious duress to fulfill a contractual obligation. After that painful experience, she became her own producer, starting with a remake of *A Star Is Born* (1976), picking Kris Kristofferson as her male lead after Elvis Presley's manager, Col. Tom Parker, refused to let his protégé share top billing. For her final project of the decade, she reteamed with *What's Up, Doc?* costar Ryan O'Neal for a battle of the sexes in *The Main Event.* As with *The Way We Were,* both films would give Streisand hits on the pop chart; "Evergreen," the theme from *A Star Is Born*, would also earn her another Academy Award, which she shared with cocomposer Paul Williams.

THE WAY WE WERE

only able to give orders to a state senator but has no qualms about ordering the murder of a judge who rules against him.

Such levels of corruption are not unusual in this type of story. In *White Line Fever* (1975), for example, a rookie independent trucker refuses to carry contraband in his rig for crooked distributors and is soon targeted by the local prosecutor on a murder frame. If there was a single aspect of civic corruption to which seventies filmmakers loved to apply themselves, however, it was the flexible relationship between bootleggers and local law enforcement in the South. In *The Last American Hero* (1973), the family patriarch knows "City Hall's so full of crooks they're falling out of the windows," and the only reason he's in jail is that he won't pay the required kickbacks. The crooked sheriff in *White Lightning* (1973) is so heavily on the take he hardly even bothers to hide it, gleefully admitting he accepts bribes delivered right to his office. The few honest sheriffs

on-screen, such as Gregory Peck's sheriff in *I Walk the Line* (1970), often find themselves facing ethical dilemmas anyway—in his case, an adulterous affair with a bootlegger's daughter forces him to suppress evidence of an escalating series of crimes. Buford Pusser of *Walking Tall* (1973) is one notable exception; his straight-arrow approach is so unusual that the criminal element feel it necessary to make an example of him through attempted murder.

WALKING TALL

Joe Don Baker created the role of Buford Pusser in the original *Walking Tall* (1973) with director Phil Karlson and writer-producer Mort Briskin, but none of them was on hand for the sequels. *Walking Tall, Part II* (1975) was supposed to star the real Sheriff Pusser, but he died in a car wreck right after signing his contract.

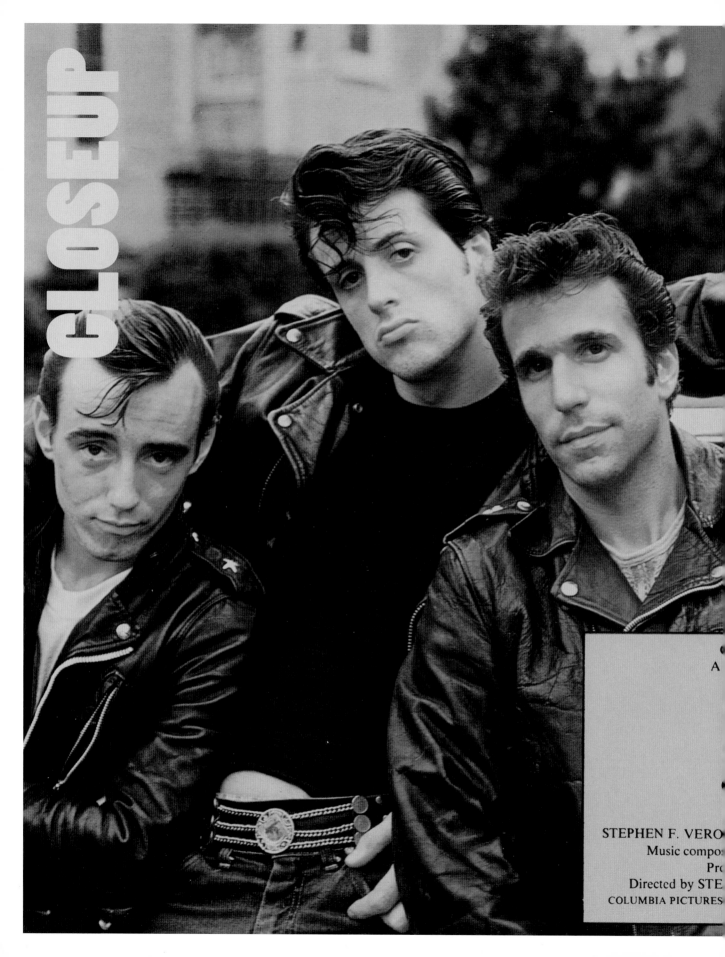

CLOSEUP

STEPHEN F. VERO
Music compo
Pr
Directed by STE
COLUMBIA PICTURES

Stephen Verona
Writer-Director

Stephen Verona spent his teen years in the 1950s in a motorcycle gang, but art classes helped lift him out of Brooklyn and into a lucrative career in advertising, including a stint as creative director at Ogilvy & Mather. In the early 1970s, he was making promotional films — prototypical music videos — for Columbia Records, and in his spare time had shot a seventeen-minute film that was nominated for an Academy Award, fueling his ambition to make a feature-length movie. His live-in girlfriend, Gayle Gleckler, provided him with more immediate inspiration to transform his adolescent memories into a screenplay: **"Quite frankly, she wouldn't screw me unless I wrote some pages. I didn't want to change my sex life, so I started pounding on the typewriter."** Gleckler would make notes on the pages as Verona submitted them to her, and in exchange for her editorial whip cracking would receive cocredit on the finished script.

Martin Davidson is also credited as a cowriter and codirector on *The Lords of Flatbush* (1974), although Verona says he didn't come onto the project until late in the game, asking to see the script during a chance meeting at a restaurant. "I was writing, producing, and directing, and I was in way over my head," Verona remembers. "I was looking for somebody to be a sounding board anyway, so I gave it to him, and he called me immediately and told me he wanted to be involved." Verona couldn't afford to pay him but was willing to hire him as a producer in exchange for the directing credit. "I thought everybody would know I was the filmmaker," Verona says. "I had no idea how important that credit was, but as a former agent, Marty knew a lot of people, and was able to use it as a stepping stone to his career."

In his original casting for the film, Verona had turned down a number of actors, including Robert De Niro and Michael Moriarty, choosing as his leads two actors who were at the time equally unknown: Sylvester Stallone and Richard Gere. Verona believes their improvisations during rehearsals led to some of the film's best dialogue, although Gere was eventually replaced in the part by Perry King — the biggest star in the production, since he had been the lead in *The Possession of Joel Delaney* (1972) — which also led to the hiring of his Yale drama school classmate, Henry Winkler. Shot mostly in late 1972 on a budget of just $161,000 — Verona avoided the expense of a union crew by claiming the film's title was *Sexual Freedom in Brooklyn*, which convinced everyone he was making a porn flick—*Lords* ultimately created a brief bidding war between studios that were eager to cash in on the post–*American Graffiti* craze for fifties nostalgia. (The two movies had been shot just six months apart in 1972; Verona knew about Lucas's film through mutual friends but drew no inspiration from it.) By the time the film premiered, in May 1974, it had another factor contributing to its box-office success: Winkler was now famous as the star of Happy Days—playing Fonzie in a style that owed much to watching his costar Stallone at work.

UMBIA PICTURES Presents
.ONA-DAVIDSON Production

"*The Lord's of Flatbush*"

Screenplay by
GAYLE GLECKER · MARTIN DAVI
rranged and conducted by JOE BROOKS
d by STEPHEN F. VERONA
N F. VERONA and MARTIN DAVIDSO
VISION OF COLUMBIA PICTURES INDUSTRIE

HORROR

THE TEXAS CHAIN SAW MASSACRE

After the box-office triumph of *The Texas Chain Saw Massacre* (1974), director Tobe Hooper tried to follow the formula of killing off strangers passing through a creepy Southern town in *Eaten Alive* (1977,
opposite), but the film fell far short of *Chainsaw*'s success, hampered by recutting (and retitling) by various distributors.

"LOOK AT ME, DAMIEN. IT'S ALL FOR YOU!" 'S ALL FOR YOU!

The corruption lurking under the surface in America's towns and cities could be metaphysical as well as institutional. While supernatural terrors were a common staple of horror films, the strict guidelines of the Hays Code meant that anything beyond the vaguest of suggestions concerning the occult was almost certainly unacceptable. With the removal of the Code's barriers, and a nudge from sophisticated British horror films such as *The Devil Rides Out* (1968), American filmmakers were able to add more details to their depic-

EATEN ALIVE

tions of the occult, especially when it came to witchcraft and devil worship (which amounted to the same thing, as far as most films from the era are concerned).

To make their staged rituals appear more authentic, many films turned to *The Satanic Bible*. Anton LaVey, the charismatic founder of the Church of Satan, published the book, actually not so much a how-to guide for black magicians as a manifesto of self-gratification, in 1969 — the same year he made a cameo appearance as the Prince of Darkness in Kenneth Anger's avant-garde short, *Invocation of My Demon Brother*. LaVey's notoriety made him semipopular among certain celebrities, but his only appearance in front of the film camera was as the high priest who runs the local coven in *The Devil's Rain* (1975), on which he also served as technical adviser. It was one of several films to use the idea of a dark cabal in an otherwise sleepy community, the most chilling of which was, perhaps, *Race with the Devil* (also 1975). It remains unclear whether that film's band of witches, stalking the vacationing couples who saw them kill a sacrificial victim, has any actual connection to the supernatural or is simply a group of murderous hooded figures bearing torches. That image can be terrifying enough, though, even if the film is set outside the South and the coven's robes aren't white.

LaVey may have popularized Satanism in the United States, but he did so by drawing upon older European traditions that had long linked the diabolism of the black mass with bourgeois decadence. American novelists ran with the idea to create their own evil hedonists, such as the wealthy apartment dwellers of Ira Levin's *Rosemary's Baby*, adapted by Roman Polanski in 1968 in his American directorial debut. Fred Mustard Stewart's first novel, *The Mephisto Waltz*, came out the following year, and veteran television producer Quinn Martin acquired the film rights soon after. The 1971 movie, which depicts a dying concert pianist's attempts to possess the body of a young man with the help of his spell-casting daughter, is full of authentic-looking occult details, but what sets *The Mephisto Waltz* apart from lesser films of the period is its knowing attitude. Brad Dillman, playing the former husband of the witchy woman, might as well be cribbing from LaVey when he dismisses their satanic rituals as merely rationalization for perversity—including an incest angle, three years before *Chinatown*, that undoubtedly explains how this Quinn Martin production evaded television-movie status and became the only theatrical release of his career.

At least one movie cult, however, had plans beyond its own pleasure. Film audiences never did learn much about the cabal that set the infernal plan depicted in *The Omen* (1976) in motion. All they could say for sure was that little Damien Thorn frightened animals and that people who took too deep an interest in him had a way of dying in mysterious circumstances. Early drafts of the screenplay had gone heavy on the supernatural imagery, but 20th Century Fox demanded a more subtle approach; thus, every death in the film, even the most outlandish accident, has a plausible explanation. But the devil's fingerprints are all over the place, if you're willing to see them, and the grisly executions, which periodically jolt the otherwise ponderous unfolding of Damien's true identity, were a hit with audiences. It eventually raked in $60 million in U.S. the-

CARRIE

Sissy Spacek was willing to let De Palma pour real pig's blood on her for the climax of *Carrie* (1976), but in the end a combination of corn syrup and food coloring proved more visually dynamic. She wore the makeup for three days straight rather than face hours of application each morning.

THE AMITYVILLE HORROR

The Amityville Horror (1979), allegedly based on a true story, inspired a string of sequels and jolted a mini-revival of haunted-house movies in the late seventies and early eighties.

ANDY WARHOL'S DRACULA

MARTIN

DRACULA

LOVE AT FIRST BITE

The old monsters of classic horror films could still send chills down filmgoers' spines. Frank Langella had done some film work in the early 1970s, but it wasn't until he re-created his Tony-nominated performance as Dracula that his movie career really took off. John Badham's 1979 adaptation of the Bram Stoker tale arrived in theaters a few months after *Love at First Bite* put a contemporary comic spin on the character as George Hamilton searches Manhattan for a new bride. (A few years earlier, David Niven had tried the same trick in London with *Old Dracula*, while Los Angeles was home to *Blacula* (1972) and *Count Yorga, Vampire* (1970), each of which spawned a sequel.) George Romero's *Martin* (1977) approached the modernization of the vampire tale from a more serious angle, abandoning the supernatural elements in order to emphasize the character's psychological alienation. Another squalid take on the legend was found in *Andy Warhol's Dracula* (1974), the first vampire film to show the effects of drinking bad blood. Like all of Warhol's movies, it was actually written and directed by Paul Morrissey, who worked closely with the artist and managed his studio for nearly a decade, continuing to make independent films after his association with Warhol ended.

aters, 10 percent of which went to Gregory Peck—making his role as Damien's adoptive father the most lucrative of his career.

William Holden was one of several actors who had turned down the lead in the first film, but Peck's financial windfall erased any qualms Holden had about playing that character's brother in *Damien: Omen II* (1978), which advances the story line seven years to the onset of the Antichrist's puberty and offers a somewhat more expansive view of the conspiracy supporting his unholy ascension. Although arguably superior to the original, the sequel ultimately did only half as well at the box office, so while producer Harvey Bernhard had plans for a seven-film epic cycle chronicling the buildup to Armageddon, the story was quickly brought to a conclusion with *The Final Conflict* (1981).

"I'M THE DEVIL. NOW, KINDLY UNDO THESE STRAPS"

Watching the devil grow up was actually more of a roller-coaster ride than an exercise in terror. The *real* horror story of the 1970s came from the devil's attempt to take over the body of a preadolescent girl in *The Exorcist* (1973). Working from William Peter Blatty's novel, which was based on an actual exorcism case, director William Friedkin methodically built up the demon's overwhelming of young Regan's personality and then set this dilemma against Father Karras's crisis of faith. The film became the year's highest-grossing movie, latching on to (and extending) the increasing public fascination with the supernatural. Along with an official sequel (1977's *Exorcist II: The Heretic*), it inspired a bevy of films involving demonic

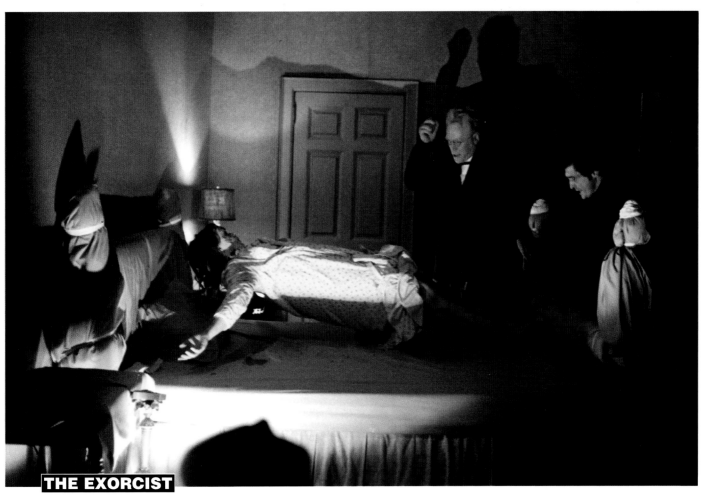

THE EXORCIST

Fathers Merrin and Karras (Max von Sydow and Jason Miller) square off against the demon possessing Regan McNeil (Linda Blair) in *The Exorcist* (1973). The exorcism alone took three months to film. When the cast and crew were not on the set, four air conditioners ran at full blast to bring the set's temperature down to 40 below; turning on the lights when the camera rolled raised the temperature to zero degrees, still cold enough to see the actors' breath when they spoke.

THE WICKER MAN

The Wicker Man (1973), starring Edward Woodward as a police inspector who uncovers a pagan cult on a remote Scottish island, is regarded as one of the most chilling horror movies of the 1970s, a reputation enhanced by years of limited availability due to the destruction of the negatives.

PHANTASM

Don Coscarelli not only wrote and directed the low-budget horror film *Phantasm* (1979), he also did the cinematography and editing. This cult favorite, in which a young boy and his brother confront an eerie undertaker with supernatural powers, seen here in a photo that creepily comes to life, went on to inspire several sequels in the eighties and nineties.

YOUNG FRANKENSTEIN

Mel Brooks, Marty Feldman, Gene Wilder, and Teri Garr during filming of his classic horror spoof *Young Frankenstein* (1974), which used the same set and props as the 1931 film starring Boris Karloff.

DAWN OF THE DEAD

It took ten years for George Romero to make a sequel to *Night of the Living Dead* (1968), and the unrelenting gore in *Dawn of the Dead* (1978) came close to earning the film an X rating.

assault or other forms of possession, including the return of dead spirits in new bodies, as seen in *The Reincarnation of Peter Proud* (1975) and *Audrey Rose* (1977).

"REMIND YOURSELF: IT'S ONLY A MOVIE"

The Exorcist also upped the stakes for haunted-house movies. *The Legend of Hell House*, which came out a few months earlier in 1973, combined elements of the old-school approaches exemplified by horror specialists American International Pictures and Britain's Hammer Films. (No surprise, as producer James H. Nicholson and writer Richard Matheson were AIP veterans, while director John Hough's previous film had been with Hammer.) Films such as *Burnt Offerings* (1976) and *The Sentinel* would begin to emphasize the visual manifestations of hauntings more prominently. *The Amityville Horror* (1979) was a notable attempt to meld the new emphasis on gross-out visuals with the psychological effects of dealing with malevolent spirits, but by the 1980s, the balance was firmly in the special-effects camp.

COMA

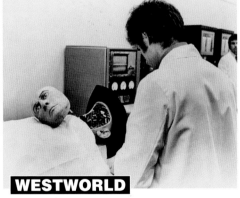

WESTWORLD

Michael Crichton (above, on the *Coma* set) wrote his first novel while he was a medical student at Harvard; the hospital thriller was filmed as *The Carey Treatment* once he'd moved to Hollywood and established himself with *The Andromeda Strain* (1971). He made his directing debut in 1973 with *Westworld*, which starred Yul Brynner as an animatronic gunslinger with a deadly malfunction that the repair crew fails to find. He was booted off his next film project, *The Terminal Man*, for diverging too far from his own story, but he would return to filmmaking four years later, writing and directing the film version of Robin Cook's *Coma*.

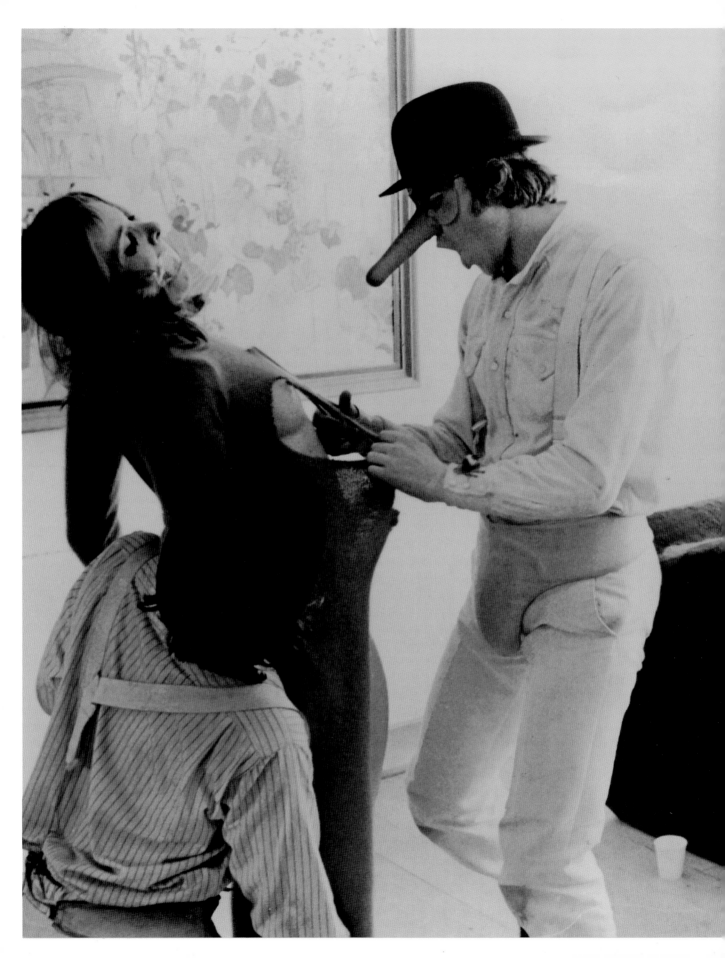

A CLOCKWORK ORANGE

Stanley Kubrick (with camera) directs Malcolm McDowell in *A Clockwork Orange* (1971). During the filming of this rape scene, McDowell's cornea was accidentally scratched, temporarily blinding him in one eye; he also suffered cracked ribs and a near drowning during the six-month shoot and to this day has a fear of eyedrops after having lived through the shooting of the brainwashing scene.

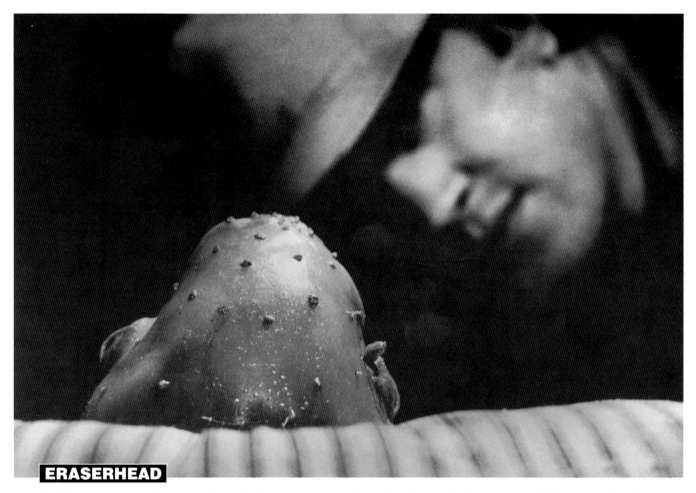

ERASERHEAD

David Lynch inspects the baby before shooting a scene from *Eraserhead* (1977). He has never publicly revealed how he created the prop, inspiring speculation that it was everything from a puppet to an embalmed cow fetus.

Not every outburst of horrific activity could be blamed on ghosts or demons: *Carrie* (1976), Brian De Palma's adaptation of the Stephen King novel, turned telekinesis into a deadly expression of teen alienation, while the monster in Larry Cohen's *It's Alive* (1974) is a mutated infant that goes on a killing spree (a B-movie counterpart, perhaps, to the deformed baby in David Lynch's painstakingly crafted 1977 debut, *Eraserhead*). And as cinematic death scenes became more spectacularly violent as the decade progressed, many films were able to generate fear without any recourse to the supernatural at all.

"MY FAMILY'S ALWAYS BEEN IN MEAT"

Wes Craven's *Last House on the Left* (1972) updated Ingmar Bergman's *The Virgin Spring*

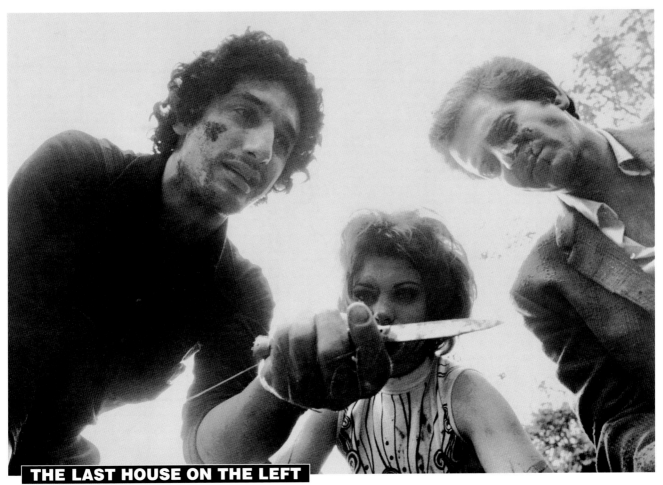

THE LAST HOUSE ON THE LEFT

Songwriter and record company executive David Hess made his acting debut as a brutal killer (wielding the knife) in *The Last House on the Left* (1972). Director Wes Craven's next flick, *The Hills Have Eyes* (1977), took the violence even further over the top, and Michael Berryman (center) became a horror icon for his role as the youngest member of a family of cannibals.

from medieval Sweden to contemporary America and added a lot more blood to the rape and murder of the teenage girls that sets the plot in motion as well as the revenge exacted by their parents. His next film, *The Hills Have Eyes* (1977), took the regional and class conflicts that had made *Deliverance* (1972) effective and added cannibalism into the mix. Meanwhile, although fledgling director Tobe Hooper tried his best to tone down the violence in *The Texas Chain Saw Massacre* (1974) for a PG rating, the film upped the ante for on-screen death, as did Bob Clark's *Black Christmas* (also 1974).

In one sense, the psychotic killers that proliferated during this decade shared a common cinematic ancestry with Norman Bates—Leatherface, the killer in *Texas Chain Saw*, was even loosely based on Ed Gein, the same killer that inspired Robert Bloch to write the

ULTRA-COOL ACTOR
DONALD PLEASENCE

"You must think me a very sinister doctor."

Donald Pleasence will always be remembered as Dr. Sam Loomis, the psychiatrist condemned to remain one step behind his most disturbed patient, Michael Myers, in *Halloween* (1978) and several of its sequels. He was not the original choice for the part—John Carpenter first approached Christopher Lee and Peter Cushing, both of whom turned him down—but he fit the role perfectly, in no small part due to a horror-film pedigree just as illustrious as his two British compatriots'. He had played a police officer chasing down a devolved killer in the London subway system in *Raw Meat* (1972), a scientist who conducts sinister experiments on his students in *The Mutations* (1973), and a retired soldier with a deadly daughter in *From Beyond the Grave* (also 1973).

But Pleasence also showed a flair for playing doctors who deal with the horrors of the modern world. In *Tales That Inspire Madness* (again 1973—a busy year, apparently) he played the head of an insane asylum in bridging sequences that introduce four short stories, a format especially popular in British horror flicks. In *The Devil Within Her* (1975), he administers to Joan Collins as she gives birth to an accursed demon baby. He would even poke fun at his own image in *Oh, God!* (1977) by playing one of the theologians convinced that John Denver's claims to have met the Almighty must be a sign of insanity.

OH, GOD!

novel *Psycho*—but plenty of room remained for variation. From the mysterious Michael Myers, who would escape at the end of *Halloween* (1978) to frighten moviegoers intermittently for more than a quarter century, to Master Sardu, the sadomasochistic villain of the ultracheap gorefest *Blood Sucking Freaks* (1976), film's violent madmen (and sometimes women) became overwhelmingly and relentlessly vicious, sometimes even outlandishly so. And although the fact that they were ultimately products of "normal" society rather than supernatural aberrations didn't necessarily make them more terrifying, it did make the best-executed films of the genre genuinely unsettling.

BLACK CHRISTMAS   **WHEN A STRANGER CALLS**   **HALLOWEEN**

Bob Clark's *Black Christmas* (1974) was one of the first "slasher movies," with an influence that was felt throughout the decade. The opening of *When a Stranger Calls* (1979) borrowed heavily from Clark's film, and conversations between Clark and John Carpenter would also guide the story line of Carpenter's *Halloween* (1978). Shot for little more than $300,000, with the actors wearing all their own clothes and the killer donning a spray-painted William Shatner mask, the film shattered box-office records for independently produced films.

CLOSEUP

Larry Cohen
Screenwriter

Larry Cohen had already directed four pictures, all of which he had written and produced as well, when he began working on the script for *God Told Me To* (1976).

Although he was best known at the time for a pair of action films starring Fred Williamson — *Black Caesar* and *Hell Up in Harlem* (both 1973) — he had recently branched out into horror with *It's Alive!* (1974). *God Told Me To* continued his exploration in the field, even as opening scenes in which a homicide detective struggles to make sense of a series of random killings make the film look much more like gritty crime drama. "I wanted the picture to look real, almost a documentary look," he recalls, "rather than artificial and overladen with special effects. I always take things from a level of believability. Instead of foisting something on the story, I ask myself what would happen if something like this really occurred. How would people react?" Cohen had not actually conceived the film's shocking second half when he wrote the first pages, he admits, "and I was always anxious to get back to work on the script so I could find out where it was going."

Tony Lo Bianco played the detective who uncovers the chilling truth about the murders — to which he has an intensely personal connection — although the film had actually begun shooting with Robert Forster in the lead. Cohen decided early on it wasn't working and shut the production down. Recalling how much he'd enjoyed working with Lo Bianco on an off-Broadway play a few years earlier, "I immediately called up Tony and told him I needed a star for my movie." Lo Bianco at once accepted what Cohen describes as "probably the best part he's ever had in his career. He's worked, still works, but he's never had anything as challenging or as broad in scope as this."

Another small but crucial role, that of a cop who snaps during New York's St. Patrick's Day Parade and starts shooting people, was played by Andy Kaufman, whom Cohen had discovered one night at the Improv. The young comedian was enthusiastic about the plan to crash the parade without obtaining filming permits. On St. Patrick's Day, Cohen inserted a uniformed Kaufman into the parade among the real officers. "They didn't say anything," the director remembers. "They saw the cameras going and thought we had permission." Three camera crews then ran up and down the parade route, setting up and breaking down at eight-block intervals to get footage of Kaufman as he marched past. The result is one of the film's most suspenseful sequences and an ongoing source of playful banter between Kaufman and Cohen. Because they had not been able to record Kaufman's one line of dialogue, "God told me to," at the parade, Cohen dubbed it in himself during postproduction. At the film's premiere, Kaufman was amazed that Cohen had been able to record him and refused to accept the explanation. "Don't tell me that," he would insist for years until his death. "I know the sound of my own voice."

Tony Lo Bianco, Deborah Raffin, and Larry Cohen (right) during filming of *God Told Me To*.

WORKING-CL

ASS HEROES

The greatest movie ever made about the television industry and its corporate venality owes its existence to a lawsuit over film profits. Screenwriter Paddy Chayefsky sued MGM over the receipts from his film *The Hospital* (1971), and in order to make the dispute disappear, the studio bought his latest script and earmarked it for production. Immediately upon its release, *Network* (1976) was acclaimed as a brilliant satire on the

NETWORK

Network (1976) was one of just a handful of movies Peter Finch shot in America during his career. He died of a stroke shortly after the film's release and became the first (and so far only) actor to win an Oscar posthumously.

lengths to which the networks would go to achieve higher ratings, but Chayefsky and director Sidney Lumet, both of whom had risen through the television ranks in the 1950s, would always insist that the film was an accurate reflection of the direction in which the industry was headed. (A little more than a quarter century later, their statements seem prophetic rather than disingenuous.)

Howard Beale, the deranged anchorman played by Peter Finch, gets most of the attention, but William Holden's portrayal of news producer Max Schumacher, forced to confront the degradation of his profession with all his faculties intact, offers an emotionally resonant portrait of a man trapped in a professional hell. He was not alone. *Save the Tiger* (1973) delves into the stirrings of conscience

SAVE THE TIGER

Jack Lemmon's gamble on *Save the Tiger* (1973) — in order to keep the film from going over budget, he took no salary —

paid off when his portrayal of a sleazy businessman on the brink of ruin won him a second Academy Award.

for a business owner for whom corruption has become a way of life. *The Candidate* (1972) shows how easy it would be for campaign consultants to transform a political neophyte into a U.S. senator, while *The Seduction of Joe Tynan* (1979) shows the compromises that would have to be made once in Congress.

It was more common, however, for Hollywood to turn to the working classes and their frustration with the system. Films such as *F.I.S.T.* (1978) and *Norma Rae* (1979) deal explicitly with workers' struggles to unionize, while *Blue Collar* (1978) suggests that even the unions themselves could be corrupted. *Car Wash* and *Mother, Jugs, and Speed* (both 1976) examine two comic facets of the labor situation in Los Angeles, while the rarely seen *Killer of Sheep* (1977) takes a much more somber view. And filmmakers discovered they could dramatize the struggle of the proletariat quite vividly by driving an eighteen-wheeler into a roadblock or a building in films such as *White Line Fever* (1975) and *Convoy* (1978).

"THEY BROUGHT THEIR FUCKING TOYS WITH THEM!"

The ongoing depiction of the working classes also influenced movies about professional and amateur athletes. Before 1970, most sports movies were either reverent biopics of legendary heroes on the level of Knute Rockne or Lou Gehrig or about men who overcame adversity to

MOTHER, JUGS & SPEED

A police officer (L. Q. Jones) checks in with Mother (Bill Cosby), Jugs (Raquel Welch), and Speed (Harvey Keitel) in Peter Yates's 1976 cynical comedy about competition between ambulance companies.

Sally Field researched her role in *Norma Rae* (1979) by working in a factory. During filming, she got so into character that in a scene where the police are trying to take her into custody, her struggling broke a rib of one of the other actors.

BLUE COLLAR

Although *Blue Collar* (1978) costars Richard Pryor (center) and Yaphet Kotto (right) argued constantly with others during filming, they were united in their frustration with Harvey Keitel (left)—and all three actors were upset with novice director Paul Schrader, who had essentially promised each that his character would be the focus of the picture.

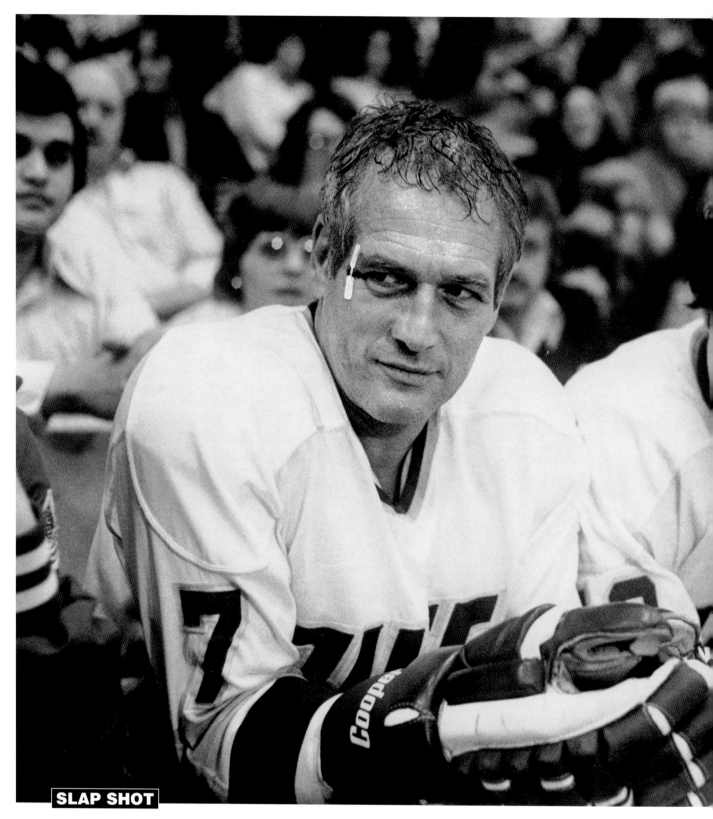

SLAP SHOT

Paul Newman's character in *Slap Shot* (1977) was almost certainly based on minor-league hockey legend John Brophy, who would later coach the Toronto Maple Leafs. Costar Michael Ontkean (center) played professional hockey to pay the tuition his senior year of college but turned down a contract offer from another NHL team to pursue an acting career.

Walter Matthau starred as an ex-ballplayer who winds up coaching a team of Little League misfits in *The Bad News Bears* (1976). The film spawned two sequels and a television series, but the only actors who came back for the later films were the kids. Jackie Earle Haley (bottom left), who played the Bears' brooding top athlete, was the only child in the cast (apart from Tatum O'Neal, far right, top) to enjoy a substantial film career afterward, including a prominent role in *Breaking Away* (1979), where he costarred with (left to right) Dennis Quaid, Daniel Stern, and Dennis Christopher.

NORTH DALLAS FORTY

Country singer Mac Davis (left) made his film debut opposite Nick Nolte as the star quarterback in *North Dallas Forty* (1979). His acting career stalled for more than a decade, though, after the producers of *The Sting II* (1983) tried to get him to fill Robert Redford's shoes.

shine on the field. The publication of *Ball Four*, major-league pitcher Jim Bouton's sex-and-drugs-filled diary of the 1969 season, changed all that, as ballplayers shifted away from being cultural heroes and became guys with jobs—better paid than most blue-collar workers, true (although this was before free agency would rocket sports salaries upward), but otherwise not so fundamentally different. The baseball team in *Bang the Drum Slowly* (1973) could be any group of workers rallying around a sick colleague in his time of need, and even the Little Leaguers in *The Bad News Bears* (1976) are scrappy underdogs refusing to accept the menial position the system has assigned to them.

A similar transformation took place in other cinematic sports. *Slap Shot* (1977) has become one of the most enthusiastically admired

THE LONGEST YARD

The supporting cast of *The Longest Yard* (1974) featured several former NFL stars, including Green Bay linebacker Ray Nitschke (left). Star Burt Reynolds played college ball for Florida State and might have gone on to the Baltimore Colts had a knee injury not sidelined his athletic career.

sports films ever made because of its no-holds-barred treatment of minor-league hockey. Novels by Dan Jenkins and Peter Gent about life in professional football led to the films *Semi-Tough* (1977) and *North Dallas Forty* (1979). Both films focus on players' exploits off the field, but *North Dallas Forty* in particular depicts its protagonist as an employee chafing under the "enlightened" management philosophy of the team's owner and coach. (His story might even be considered a more realistic variation on that of Jonathan E., the *Rollerball* all-star who becomes targeted for death after he refuses to retire when he's supposed to.) *The Longest Yard* (1974) uses football's brutality to probe the relationship between convicts and the prison system, while *Heaven Can Wait* (1978) takes a more sentimental approach to the game in a literal sports fantasy.

KANSAS CITY BOMBER

Raquel Welch produced *Kansas City Bomber* (1972) as part of the effort to reverse the damage done by *Myra Breckinridge* (1970). After accepting the script hand delivered to her by an aspiring film student, she did most of her own skating for the film and broke her wrist during shooting.

ROLLERBALL

The cast and stunt crew of *Rollerball* (1975) took to the futuristic sport so readily that they would actually play it for fun between scenes.

FAST BREAK

THE FISH THAT SAVED PITTSBURGH

In 1979, Gabe Kaplan and Stockard Channing starred in separate basketball movies that revolved around turning a bunch of misfits into a winning team: *Fast Break* and *The Fish That Saved Pittsburgh*, respectively. Although the methods of Channing's astrologer character were more unorthodox, she had the edge on talent, even over superstar Julius Erving.

Goldengirl (1979) presents an equally fantastic, though much less optimistic, picture of Olympic track-and-field competition—a far cry from Michael Winner's attempt in *The Games* (1970) to meld a realistic depiction of marathon training with the melodramatic approach to auto-racing matches typically used in films such as *Le Mans* (1971). The star of that film, Steve McQueen, also lent his talents that year to an Oscar-nominated documentary, *Any Given Sunday*, which explores the world of off-road motorcycle racing.

"APOLLO CREED MEETS THE ITALIAN STALLION"

If seventies filmmakers focused particularly on any one sport, though, it would almost certainly be boxing. It had always been a favorite subject for the movies: a visually dynamic activity confined to a small physical space, a sport that literalized the metaphor of being beaten down by life while providing an arena in which underdogs could triumph by sheer tenacity. But the attention paid to the sport in this decade was slightly different and was influenced, in part, by events in the real world. The fame of Muhammad Ali—first for his rise through the ranks of professional boxing and then for his controversial acceptance of the Nation of Islam and rejection of the U.S. military draft—made him (along with his outsize personality) a natural for the movies. When he was effectively banned from competition for his conscientious objection to the war in Vietnam, he appeared in the documentary *A.K.A. Cassius Clay* (1970) to offer running commentary on the

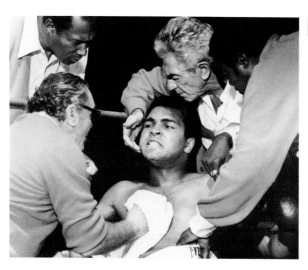

THE GREATEST

Muhammad Ali had been the subject of numerous documentaries, but in *The Greatest* (1977), he starred as himself in a fictional retelling of his early career. The film's all-star cast included Ernest Borgnine as Angelo Dundee, Ali's trainer, and John Marley as a ringside doctor.

ROCKY

John Avildsen and crew film Sylvester Stallone in the early stages of Rocky Balboa's training. Note the Steadicam; *Rocky* (1976) was the first Hollywood picture to use the camera for extensive principal photography.

FAT CITY

A boxer on his way down (Stacy Keach) meets one on his way up (Jeff Bridges) and is inspired to climb into the ring again himself in John Huston's *Fat City* (1972).

RAGING BULL

The string of boxing movies in the 1970s hit its apex with *Raging Bull* (1980). When people think of the lengths to which Robert De Niro went for the film, they usually think of the sixty-five-pound weight gain. But to play boxer Jake La Motta in his prime, the star also underwent a heavy training regimen and then entered—and won—actual amateur boxing matches in Brooklyn.

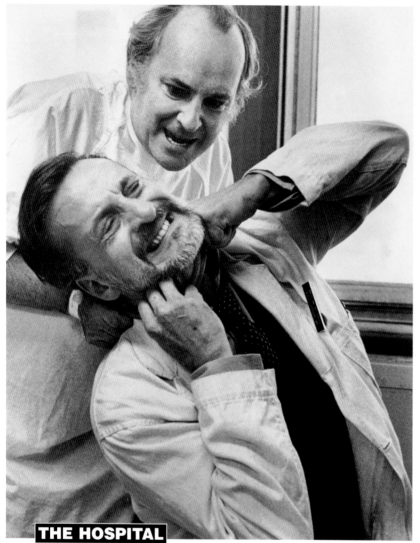

THE HOSPITAL

George C. Scott's problems catch up with him in *The Hospital* (1971). Not having learned their lesson from the year before, when Scott had rejected the Oscar for *Patton*, the Academy went ahead and nominated him for the best actor award again.

FREEBIE AND THE BEAN

As the lead roles in *Freebie and the Bean* (1974), James Caan and Alan Arkin play two San Francisco cops who take Dirty Harry's unrestrained approach to law enforcement to comic extremes. It was only Richard Rush's second big studio picture after working for American International and other low-budget producers. A conflict with 20th Century Fox over his next film, *The Stunt Man* (1980), kept it out of circulation for two years.

THE NEW CENTURIONS

A rookie cop (Stacy Keach) restrains an abusive mother while his partner (George C. Scott) protects her infant child in a scene from *The New Centurions* (1972), based on author Joseph Wambaugh's own experiences on the Los Angeles police force.

heavyweight champions of the past. Seven years later, he became one of a handful of people to star as themselves in the movie of their life when *The Greatest* dramatized those controversies and his comeback fights leading up to the famous "Rumble in the Jungle" against George Foreman.

Although a few notable boxing films were made in the first half of the seventies, such as *Fat City* (1972) and *The All-American Boy* (1973), the film everybody remembers is *Rocky* (1976). Sylvester Stallone was still a struggling actor when he watched an unknown boxer named Chuck Wepner go the distance with Ali and, inspired by the fight, devoted a three-day creative frenzy to a screenplay about a working-class Philadelphian who gets a shot at the heavyweight title. He cannily sold the script on the condition that he would be cast as Rocky Balboa, which worried the producers so much that they agreed on the condition that director John G. Avildsen bring the film in on a budget of only $1 million. (The final cost went slightly over.) In the end, though, Stallone's persistence was

KLUTE

Bree Daniels (Jane Fonda) surveys her ransacked apartment in a scene from *Klute* (1971). After Barbra Streisand turned down the part of a New York prostitute who develops a relationship with a private eye trying to track one of her former customers, Fonda took it and won the first of her two Oscars.

"I find your lack of faith disturbing."

James Earl Jones first made it big in the New York theater world in a 1961 production of Jean Genet's *The Blacks*, where he starred alongside Roscoe Lee Browne, Raymond St. Jacques, Cicely Tyson, Godfrey Cambridge, and Maya Angelou. He began collecting awards for his off-Broadway roles and then won his first Tony for performing as Jack Jefferson in Howard Sackler's *The Great White Hope*, a fictionalization of the life of Jack Johnson, the black heavyweight boxing champion of the early twentieth century who became a focal point for American racism. He reprised the role in the 1970 film version of the play. It was not his first film role—he had a minor part as a member of the flight crew in *Dr. Strangelove* (1964) and had reunited with many of his costars from *The Blacks* on the set of *The Comedians* (1967)—but it was the first time he'd starred in a picture, and he received an Academy Award nomination in recognition of his talent.

The film roles immediately following would demonstrate Jones's dramatic range, as he moved effortlessly from the nation's first black president in *The Man* (1972) to a trash collector who woos a single mother in *Claudine* (1974). He was one of several African-American stars, including Billy Dee Williams and Richard Pryor, to team up on *The Bingo Long Traveling All-Stars & Motor Kings* (1976), a humorous story about black ballplayers in the days before pro ball was integrated, and he would also appear opposite Muhammad Ali in *The Greatest* (1977), as civil rights leader Malcolm X. But his most famous role from the seventies is the one in which he is only heard, never seen, as the voice of Darth Vader in *Star Wars* (also 1977). He was uncredited at his own request.

THE GREAT WHITE HOPE

justified, as the film won both best picture and best director Academy Awards, along with a prize for editing. It was nominated for seven other Oscars: Stallone was nominated for both the screenplay and his portrayal of Rocky, while fellow cast members Talia Shire, Burgess Meredith, and Burt Young would also earn recognition from the Academy. (The instantly recognizable theme song composed by Bill Conti, "Gonna Fly Now," was nominated but lost out to Barbra Streisand's rendition of "Evergreen," from *A Star Is Born*.)

The film's remarkable success drove plans for a sequel that Stallone would direct as well as write and star in, but it also had other filmmakers scrambling to come up with their own boxing stories. *Rocky II* was released in 1979, when it faced competition from Franco Zeffirelli's melodramatic remake of *The Champ*, Ryan O'Neal and Barbra Streisand reunion for *The Main Event*, Ron O'Neal knocking his opponents senseless in *The Hitter*, and Tim Conway bumbling through *The Prize Fighter* with Don Knotts for moral support. The outcome was never in doubt.

THE EYES OF LAURA MARS

Faye Dunaway starred in *The Eyes of Laura Mars* (1978) as a fashion photographer who has psychic visions from the perspective of a serial killer. Several of Laura's photos based on these visions, an unsettling blend of eroticism and violent content, were shot by acclaimed photographer Helmut Newton.

ON THE ROAD

THE SUGARLAND EXPRESS

Although the TV-movie *Duel* had been released theatrically in Europe, *The Sugarland Express* (1974) was Steven Spielberg's first motion picture directing assignment. When filming was completed, he bought the car in which he had spent weeks filming Goldie Hawn, William Atherton, and Michael Sacks as a personal memento.

HARRY & TONTO

Art Carney won an Oscar for *Harry & Tonto* (1974), Paul Mazursky's story of an elderly man's cross-country journey from New York to Los Angeles (with his pet cat in tow).

After the phenomenal popularity of *Easy Rider* in the summer of 1969, playing to the counterculture was widely regarded as a guarantee for similar box-office success. MGM brought Michelangelo Antonioni to the United States to shoot *Zabriskie Point* (1970) in the California desert, while Tom Laughlin made the Southwest safe for horses and hippies in *Billy Jack* (1971) and Robert Redford and Michael J. Pollard played an unlikely pair of motorcycle racers in *Little Fauss and Big Halsy* (1970). *Vanishing Point* and *Two-Lane Blacktop* (both 1971) may do the most effective job of emulating the antiestablishment attitude of *Easy Rider*. *Vanishing Point*, with a pseudonymous screenplay by avant-garde novelist G. Cabrera Infante, matched and even surpassed *Easy Rider*'s

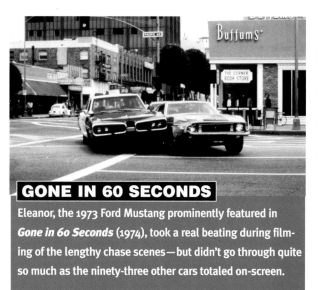

GONE IN 60 SECONDS

Eleanor, the 1973 Ford Mustang prominently featured in *Gone in 60 Seconds* (1974), took a real beating during filming of the lengthy chase scenes—but didn't go through quite so much as the ninety-three other cars totaled on-screen.

nihilistic ending, while *Two-Lane Blacktop* nails the aimless narrative aspect as it follows two cars racing each other across the country.

In the long run, however, it was enough for films to simply give chase on the open road, and the buddy pairing of Dennis Hopper and Peter Fonda eventually gave way to more conventional romantic duos in films such as *Badlands* (1973), *Dirty Mary, Crazy Larry* (1974), and *Aloha, Bobby and Rose*

(1975). (Conventional in their configuration, that is, not in their action.) Ron Howard made his directing debut with *Grand Theft Auto* (1977), a romantic comedy produced by Roger Corman that piles on the car crashes, just as Steven Spielberg's first major projects, the TV-movie *Duel* and *The Sugarland Express* (1974), are both car chases—though admittedly of a very different sort. With *Smokey and the Bandit*, Burt Reynolds and Sally Field take car-bound romance to new heights, leading Clint Eastwood to tackle the genre with *his* girlfriend, Sondra Locke, in *Every Which Way But Loose* (1978). (Both would continue their franchises into the next decade.)

"THIS MEANS SOMETHING. THIS IS IMPORTANT"

The greater influence of the road picture, however, would be felt throughout Hollywood. *Easy Rider* can't be given all the credit for this; after all, sending characters out on the open road had been a proven formula for success at least as far back as Claudette Colbert and Clark Gable's misadventures in *It Happened One Night* or Bob Hope and Bing Crosby's escapades on the road to one foreign country after another. But during the 1970s, an explicit quality defined the journeys that was stronger than it had ever been before. When characters such as those played by Al Pacino and Gene Hackman in *Scarecrow* (1973) or Art Carney in *Harry & Tonto* (1974) made their way across the country, they were looking to restore meaning to the lives that had been pulled out from under them. The navy sailors escorting their prisoner to the stockades in *The Last Detail* (1973) may try to comfort themselves that they're only doing their job, but their trek up the eastern seaboard forces them to recognize their own situation just as they've tried to educate their young charge about life.

BEING THERE

Peter Sellers (right) plays a gardener whose banal, TV-influenced "wisdom" is taken up by the U.S. president (Jack Warden) in Hal Ashby's satirical *Being There* (1979).

OH, GOD!

It was twenty years before John Denver acted in another movie after *Oh, God!* (1977), but George Burns would go on to play the Supreme Being in two sequels (the last of which also featured him as the devil).

THE JERK

In 1979, Steve Martin was a successful stand-up comedian with small cameos in two films, but *The Jerk* (1979) instantly transformed him into a movie star.

248 the stewardess is flying the plane!

BADLANDS

The law catches up with Kit and Holly (Martin Sheen and Sissy Spacek) at the end of *Badlands* (1973). Former MIT philosophy professor Terrence Malik's debut film was shot in Colorado for about $500,000; he made one more movie in the seventies and then let twenty years pass before he made another picture.

The motif cannot be confined to any one genre but extends through all of them. In order to make sense of his UFO sighting in *Close Encounters of the Third Kind*, Richard Dreyfuss needs to make his way to Wyoming. Jack Lemmon tries to hold his sanity together while wandering through New York in *The Out-of-Towners* and Los Angeles in *Save the Tiger*. *Apocalypse Now* is a long trek up a river into the heart of darkness, while *The In-Laws* takes a different approach to teaching its protagonist that the world is insane. Even *The Muppet Movie* presents a voyage of discovery, with Kermit the Frog acquiring his familiar companions as he makes his way from his swampy home to Hollywood to become the movie star he knows he was meant to be.

These journeys mirror a national soul-searching that had begun with the more active members of the counterculture in the sixties (and even earlier, in some cases). By the 1970s,

LITTLE FAUSS AND BIG HALSY

Little Fauss and Big Halsy (1970) costars Michael J. Pollard and Robert Redford weren't faking their on-screen personality clash. Although the film was not a hit, producers Albert S. Ruddy and Gray Frederickson had much better luck with a later project: ***The Godfather***.

THE MUPPET MOVIE

The Muppet Movie's star, Kermit the Frog (with his creator, Jim Henson, top left), appeared with several Hollywood stars, including Madeline Kahn, Steve Martin, and Paul Williams. Charles Durning played the film's villain, frog-leg entrepreneur Doc Hopper, while Orson Welles appeared at the end as film producer Lew Lord, an in-joke reference to the film's producer, Sir Lew Grade.

Mark Hamill's first movie after *Star Wars* was *Corvette Summer* (1978), a romantic comedy about a high-school student and a novice prostitute (Annie Potts) who meet while hunting down his stolen car.

CORVETTE SUMMER

THE VAN

The title attraction in *The Van* (1977) had all the right features for the late seventies—an eight-track player, shag carpeting, a water bed, even a mirrored ceiling—but the film is chiefly remembered today for the presence of Danny DeVito (not shown here) in the supporting cast. Stuart Goetz (leaning against the Straight Arrow) acted in only one other movie after this before taking up a new career as a music editor for film and television, where he's worked on shows such as *Sports Night* and *The West Wing*.

PAPER MOON

At ten, Tatum O'Neal was the youngest actress ever to win an Academy Award in competition for her performance in *Paper Moon* (1973) in which she costarred with her father, Ryan O'Neal (right). The movie was turned into a sitcom starring Jodie Foster that lasted for only thirteen episodes before being canceled.

all Americans were forced to ask themselves and each other hard questions about the direction of their individual and national lives. For some filmmakers, that meant directly confronting the status quo. Some placed their emphasis on depicting life's experiences with an unflinching honesty. Others piled adversity onto their characters to demonstrate human resilience . . . or to warn that an insurmountable danger might be imminent. And yet others were simply out to offer audiences a few hours of escape. Almost all of them, though, worked within the system—aiming not to overthrow Hollywood but to find, or keep, their own place within it. Angry young filmmakers got most of the attention and acclaim,

TWO-LANE BLACKTOP

Months before the movie's release, *Esquire* declared that *Two-Lane Blacktop* (1971), starring musicians Dennis Wilson (center) and James Taylor (right), was going to be "the film of the year." Their cross-country race against GTO-driving Warren Oates (left) tanked in theaters but has become an underground classic.

CANNONBALL

After the success of *Death Race 2000* (1975), David Carradine reunited with director Paul Bartel for another high-speed cross-country race in *Cannonball* (1976). The film featured cameo appearances by producer Roger Corman and fellow directors Allan Arkush, Joe Dante, and Martin Scorsese.

VANISHING POINT

Kowalski takes his car off-road to evade the police in *Vanishing Point* (1971). Barry Newman did most of his own driving during the shoot, although slowing down the cameras meant that he didn't have to drive quite as fast as he appeared to be on-screen.

ULTRA-COOL ACTOR
WARREN OATES

"If I'm not grounded pretty soon, I'm going to go into orbit."

Warren Oates will always be associated with the Westerns, especially with the films of Sam Peckinpah, with whom he first worked in 1962's *Ride the High Country*. But in the 1970s, Oates began to move beyond the genre and would play an integral part in the transformation of the road picture from escapist action to existential statement.

Monte Hellman put Oates behind the wheel of a GTO in *Two-Lane Blacktop* (1971), and the actor's twang is perfect for the part of the loquacious driver who can't stop enthusing about how great his car is and spinning yarns about his life, his constant chatter counterpointing the sullen silences from James Taylor and Dennis Wilson. That same year, Oates costarred with Peter Fonda in *The Hired Hand*, a western with a plot structure that borrowed heavily from the wandering format of *Easy Rider* (1969).

After making five films in 1973, including a small role as Holly's father in *Badlands*, Oates found two films in 1974 that were just as perfect for him as *Two-Lane Blacktop* had been. He went back to work for Hellman in *Cockfighter*, where he barely says a word throughout the entire picture as he travels from one cockfight to the next looking for a shot at the title. He also reteamed with Peckinpah in *Bring Me the Head of Alfredo Garcia*, playing a barfly who takes it upon himself to collect the bounty on a man who's already dead. The director's usual fixation on savage violence, combined with huge swaths of black humor, enables Oates to give an expansive performance (some might say outlandish) that has come to be regarded as his star turn.

BRING ME THE HEAD OF ALFREDO GARCIA

but experienced veterans with twenty or more years' experience in the industry were more than capable of adapting to new standards of suitable subject matter and acceptable levels of frankness. Some of them embraced the new freedoms and even outpaced their younger colleagues, while others took more reactionary stances. Hollywood had room for all of them, so long as, whatever they wanted to talk about in their movies, the writers and directors remembered that the ultimate purpose of filmmaking was to entertain crowds and to make money.

SMOKEY AND THE BANDIT

The real-life romance between Burt Reynolds and Sally Field (seen here with costar Jerry Reed) helped *Smokey and the Bandit* outpace nearly all its competition at the movies. Only *Star Wars* would make more at the box office in 1977.

"The most important thing Roger [Corman] did for me was sit down with me right before I directed *Caged Heat* [1974] and run down just how to do a job of moviemaking. He hit everything: Have something interesting in the foreground of the shot; have something interesting happening in the background of the shot; try to find good motivation to move the camera, because it's more stimulating to the eyes; if you're shooting the scene in a small room where you can't move the camera, try to get different angles, because cuts equal movement; respect the characters and try to like them, and translate that into the audience liking and respecting the characters. To me, those are the fundamentals. I don't know if Roger had a similar lunch with Coppola, but look at *The Godfather*. It's a classical Roger Corman movie. All the Corman moves are there — a little sex, a little violence, a little social comment."

— Jonathan Demme, 1984

BLOODY MAMA

Roger Corman illustrates the proper technique for shooting out of a car window during a getaway on the set of ***Bloody Mama*** (1970). After directing this film, Corman spent most of the decade as a producer, overseeing early films by acclaimed filmmakers such as Martin Scorsese, Jonathan Demme, Ron Howard, and John Sayles.

Faye Dunaway in *Chinatown* (1974)

A NOTE ON THE PHOTOGRAPHY

If you were a child or teenager in America during the 1970s, you have probably noticed that most, if not all, of your color class pictures or family portraits have somewhat faded and turned magenta or pinkish/reddish over time. This can often come as quite a shock, especially when compared to some types of color photography from the decades before the 1970s, which have proved to be far more stable and durable. This phenomenon is not isolated to personal photos from the 1970s; it has stretched to every form of media, film, and advertising from that specific time period.

One of the most significant problems film preservationists face today is the deterioration of color motion-picture film not yet even forty years old. How is this possible? How can a film such as *Taxi Driver* (1976) need more preservation work than *West Side Story* (1961)? Simple. The demand for easier, faster, and cheaper often overrode any thoughts of future preservation. The inferior quality of film stock, combined with faster, less archival film processing, left their reddened mark, and many films from this time period now often appear muddy, faded, or discolored. Sometimes this effect was planned, as in the cases of *McCabe & Mrs. Miller* (1971) and *The Godfather* (1972), which utilize a reddened or sepia-toned palette. But more often than not, most films from this decade are merely a shadow of their former glory. Fortunately, due in most part to innovative, digital preservation techniques, many of these films are being preserved (albeit expensively) with most of their original color restored.

Strange as it may sound, it is far easier to illustrate a book on film history pre-1970 than post-1970. This is mainly because of the way studios chose to promote their films in the 1970s. Up until the 1950s, most studios and their photographers used large-format negatives (8 x 10 and 4 x 5) during filming to produce their stills. By the 1970s, 35mm photography had become the new industry standard, until the recent advent of digital photography. Even though the 35mm had the advantage of being faster and more economical, the quality produced from the larger-format negatives was far superior due to the size and the ability to capture more detail. In the 1970s, the majority of motion pictures were filmed in color, but most newspapers were printed in black and white. The studios did not see the use in issuing color photographs for publicity, so the majority of unit still photography was taken in black and white.

Today, most magazines, books, and newspapers expect color photography from films shot in color. This has become quite a challenge for films of the 1970s. Color-unit still photographs taken on the sets of the motion pictures not only are scarce, but the same problems with film also apply to photographs — the colors muddy and fade, and preservation is needed to restore and stabilize the original colors.

The lack of locatable, true, still photographic images explains why so many frame enlargements (film frames from the motion picture itself) are used in books. For this project, great efforts were made to find actual photographs and slides — no frame enlargements were used. Each image chosen was also painstakingly digitally restored to the closest approximation of its original color. For the first time, readers have the best possible look at the true still photography of the fascinating cinematic decade of the 1970s.

—Manoah Bowman, Photo Editor

TAGLINES

A key to the quotes used throughout the book

"The force is strong with this one."
Star Wars (1977)

"Have you recently had a close encounter?"
Close Encounters of the Third Kind (1977)

"The only good human . . . is a dead human!"
Planet of the Apes (1968)

"Sorry the world didn't make it."
Omega Man (1971)

"There is no renewal!"
Logan's Run (1976)

"Remind me to send a thank-you note to Mister Boeing."
Airport (1970)

"For God's sake, reverend, what you're doing is suicide!"
The Poseidon Adventure (1972)

"Stay out of the water!"
Jaws (1975)

"The sudden decompression at 30,000 feet is something you gotta see to believe."
Airport (1970)

"This isn't a hospital; it is an insane asylum!"
*M*A*S*H* (1970)

"The Nazis are the enemy. Wade into them."
Patton (1970)

"Saigon—shit, I'm still only in Saigon."
Apocalypse Now (1979)

"I love the smell of napalm in the morning."
Apocalypse Now (1979)

"Forget it, Jake, it's Chinatown."
Chinatown (1974)

"It leads everywhere. Get out your notebooks."
All the President's Men (1976)

"I'm not afraid of death, but I am afraid of murder."
The Conversation (1974)

"I was born game and I intend to go out that way."
True Grit (1969)

"History is nothing more than disrespect for the dead."
Buffalo Bill and the Indians (1976)

"Excuse me while I whip this out."
Blazing Saddles (1974)

"Dying ain't much of a living."
The Outlaw Josey Wales (1976)

"I believe only in dynamite."
Duck, You Sucker (aka *A Fistful of Dynamite*, 1971)

"Now, how do you want to work this?"
The Sting (1973)

"What do you think this is, a Western?"
Silver Streak (1976)

"I'm robbing a bank because they got money here."
Dog Day Afternoon (1975)

"This game is called survival. Let's see how well you can play it."
Women in Cages (1971)

"Hey, you bastards, I'm still here."
Papillon (1973)

"In the water I'm a very skinny lady."
The Poseidon Adventure (1972)

"Don't ever take sides with anyone against the family."
The Godfather (1972)

"You've got to ask yourself one question: Do I feel lucky?"
Dirty Harry (1971)

"You don't make up for your sins in church."
Mean Streets (1973)

"I know it was you, Fredo."
The Godfather (1972)

"Wilkommen, bienvenue, welcome."
Cabaret (1972)

"It's showtime, folks."
All That Jazz (1979)

"My purpose in coming to Hollywood is the destruction of the American male in all its particulars."
Myra Breckinridge (1970)

"Life is a cabaret, old chum."
Cabaret (1972)

"That was the most fun I've ever had without laughing."
Annie Hall (1977)

"You're a funny man, Al. A pain in the ass, but a funny man."
The Sunshine Boys (1975)

"I'm all dressed up and ready to fall in love!"
Pink Flamingos (1972)

"We've had nice talking, now we're going to have door breaking."
Plaza Suite (1971)

"Nothing's really been right since Sam the Lion died."
The Last Picture Show (1971)

"You want me to drive to Texarkana, pick up four hundred cases of Coors, and come back in twenty-eight hours? No problem."
Smokey and the Bandit (1977)

"Look at me, Damien. It's all for you!"
The Omen (1976)

"I'm the Devil. Now, kindly undo these straps."
The Exorcist (1973)

"Remind yourself: It's only a movie."
The Last House on the Left (1972)

"My family's always been in meat."
The Texas Chain Saw Massacre (1974)

"You must think me a very sinister doctor."
Halloween (1978)

UP IN SMOKE

"Hey, I got something for ya, lardass!"

"I'm mad as hell, and I'm not going to take this anymore."
Network (1976)

"They brought their fucking toys with them!"
Slap Shot 1977)

"Apollo Creed meets the Italian Stallion."
Rocky (1976)

"I find your lack of faith disturbing."
Star Wars (1977)

"The last beautiful free soul on this planet."
Vanishing Point (1971)

"This means something. This is important."
Close Encounters of the Third Kind (1977)

"If I'm not grounded pretty soon, I'm going to go into orbit."
Two-Lane Blacktop (1971)

ACKNOWLEDGMENTS

Let's get the most important thing out of the way first: There is no way this book can even come close to being genuinely comprehensive, and as a result at least one of your favorite films is missing. I feel your pain, because I had to leave out some of my favorites, too. And some of my editor's favorites, and some of my photo editor's favorites—you should have heard him demanding to know why we weren't even asking for pictures from some films.

As long as I am talking about my photo editor, though, this book would not be as amazing as it is without Manoah Bowman's diligent work. More than once, I was convinced he wouldn't be able to find anything at all on some obscure film, but he always came through. Thanks also to Jennifer Kita, his patient assistant, who had to catalogue and organize the hundreds of photos and slides, which Robert Cushman at the Academy of Motion Picture Arts and Sciences was kind enough to make available from the photo archives, and to Dolly and Laurel at Jerry Ohlinger's in Manhattan, who came through in the clutch with some last-minute additions to the visual lineup.

Also, for the record, the design work by Roger Gorman and his crew at Reiner Deisgn totally rocks, and the production team at Bulfinch, Denise LaCongo and Pamela Schechter, has done a great job of making that design and the images look fantastic.

These contributions to the visual component of this book are essential, but *The Stewardess Is Flying the Plane!* simply wouldn't exist without ace editor Karyn Gerhard. The basic idea of a 1970s film survey was all hers, and the structure of this book—and its selection of films—came about after weeks of intense editorial collaboration and negotiation. I'm pretty much running with the ball she handed off to me, but all the opinions are entirely my own responsibility. (Karyn also loaned me several films from her own collection, and set me up with Gideon Dabi, who let me borrow even more.)

Thanks go to everyone else at Bulfinch who helped steer this through, including publisher Jill Cohen, publicist Matthew Ballast, and assistant Alex Logan.

Thanks to Mark Sarvas for providing me with crash space when I had to do research in Los Angeles, and to John Anderson and James Highfill for letting me sleep on their couch when the research was done—and for a conversation about movies (not just '70s flicks) that has lasted more than a dozen years despite all too many interruptions. I wouldn't be able to talk movies with them nearly as intelligently if it hadn't been for the film studies faculty of the University of Notre Dame in the early '90s—Jim Collins, Ava Preacher Collins, Hilary Radner, and James Petersen—and then at USC Cinema-Television, especially Rick Jewell and Todd Boyd.

Special thanks to Larry Cohen, Dan O'Bannon, and Stephen Verona for taking the time to tell me their stories, and an extra-special thanks to Peter Bogdanovich for a wonderful (and all too short) conversation that helped put many of the ideas I'd had swirling around my head into perspective.

Leslie Daniels came into my life just when I needed a literary agent, and I'm looking forward to working with her on many books to follow.

Thanks to Psyche and Clotilde for relenting in their demands to be fed and/or petted long enough for me to get the writing done, and extra-special thanks to Laura for allowing me to hog all the space on the TiVo for months on end . . . along with everything else she means to me, which could fill up a book of its own.

Ron Hogan
December 2004

Elaine May directing
A New Leaf 1971

A special thank-you to the following: assistant photographic editor Jennifer Kita for managing and tirelessly organizing all of the photographs appearing in this book and for her excellence and dedication in the pursuit of perfection; AMPAS photographic curator Robert Cushman for his continued support, knowledge, and most of all his generosity; photographer and photographic preservationist Shane McCauley, who painstakingly digitally restored and color corrected all of the photographs seen herein; Bulfinch editor Karyn Gerhard for her amazing ability to turn her inspirations into realities, no longer an easy feat in the ever-changing world of publishing; Matthew Tunia for providing some essential never-before-seen images from his archive that help make this book as special as it is; and Tom Wilson for his film knowledge and eagle eye during the initial photographic selection. Finally, acknowledgments would not be complete without a thank-you to the following: Tony Maietta, Erin Kita, Brett Davidson, Matthew Seckman, Anna Hrnjak, Ann Jastrab, Laurent Bouzereau, Jay Jorgensen, Sue Gulden, and Stephen Tapert.

Manoah Bowman, Photo Editor

INDEX

Italic page numbers refer to illustrations.

Bulfinch Press

Time Warner Book Group
1271 Avenue of the Americas, New York, NY 10020
Visit our Web site at www.bulfinchpress.com

First Edition: November 2005

Library of Congress Cataloging-in-Publication Data
Hogan, Ron.
The stewardess is flying the plane!: American films of the 1970s /
Ron Hogan; Manoah Bowman, photo editor; conversation with Peter
Bogdanovich. — 1st ed.
p. cm.
ISBN 0-8212-5751-X
1. Motion pictures — United States — History. I. Bowman, Manoah. II. Title.
PN1993.5.U6H57 2005
791.43'0973'09047–dc22   2005002337

Design by Roger Gorman, Reiner Design Consultants, Inc.

PRINTED IN HONG KONG